EVERYDAY GUIDES
MADE EASY

MICROSOFT
OFFICE
BASICS

ROGER LAING

FLAME TREE
PUBLISHING

CONTENTS

Find out about the various Office programs and how to work with
them on your desktop, tablet and smartphone, as well as online.

Get started with quick techniques for creating, formatting,
editing and printing great-looking documents.

See how to use Excel to store and organize your data and work with
calculations and charts.

As well as being your personal email service, Outlook
lets you arrange your time, contacts and calendar.

Here are the tips to make your presentations dynamic and fun.

Discover OneNote to have your notes with you wherever you are, Publisher for
professional-looking publications and Access for creating desktop databases.

FOREWORD

Windows, launched in 1985, began as a way to navigate PCs without having to resort to command prompts, and, although early versions might look clunky by today's standards, the concept of navigating a computer through 'windows' rather than through hard-to-remember commands immediately caught on. Millions of installs later, Windows is the most popular computer operating system on the planet, with more than 1.25 billion PCs running a version of Windows today.

To complement Windows in the business space, Microsoft developed Microsoft Office back in 1990, and without Office programs like Word, Excel and Powerpoint our world would look very different today.

This guide to Microsoft Office is designed to take you from zero to hero without any of the pain; but fear not, we won't bamboozle you with jargon. We'll mainly cover the basics of this feature-rich software, progressing through to some slightly more advanced functions. Each chapter has a number of Hot Tips that'll ensure you're on the very cutting edge without breaking a sweat.

This step-by-step guide is written by an expert on Microsoft Office, so you can be sure of the best advice, and is suitable for anyone from the complete beginner through to slightly more advanced users who would like a refresher. You'll find this guide an excellent reference volume on Office, and it will grace your bookcase for years to come.

Mark Mayne Editor of T3.com

INTRODUCTION

Microsoft Office is a combination of applications for everyday needs – from Word for word processing to Outlook for email and Excel for budgets and calculations – that can be used on your computer, mobile or online. This book explains how to use them to best advantage.

NEED TO KNOW

This book is full of practical techniques and tips to help you get started with Office programs, as well as looking at more advanced features – such as text effects in Word or animations in PowerPoint – to help you become more proficient.

SMALL CHUNKS

Every chapter is written in a concise way, describing particular features within the various Office programs and how to use them. Instead of reading from start to finish, just dip into the sections you need.

> ### Hot Tips
>
> **All the way through, Hot Tips show the many shortcuts and quick techniques available in Office programs.**

STEP-BY-STEP GUIDES

Follow the instructions to complete a variety of tasks in Office, from adding a chart in Excel to inserting a transition between slides in PowerPoint.

SIX CHAPTERS

There are six chapters in this book. The first looks at all the programs that make up the Office suite and the different versions for use on your computer, mobile device or online. The second covers quick and easy techniques for getting started with Word, including creating, formatting, editing and printing documents. The third chapter shows how to use Excel for storing and organizing your data – then using it for calculations or creating charts. The next chapter has useful tips on getting organized with Outlook, whether it's handling your email on the computer or online, adding contacts, or setting up calendars and tasks. The fifth explains how to create and edit PowerPoint presentations, adding transition effects and animations to make them more dynamic and fun. The final chapter looks at other Office programs, including OneNote for note-taking – on the computer and on the go – Publisher for creating great-looking publications and Access for setting up desktop databases.

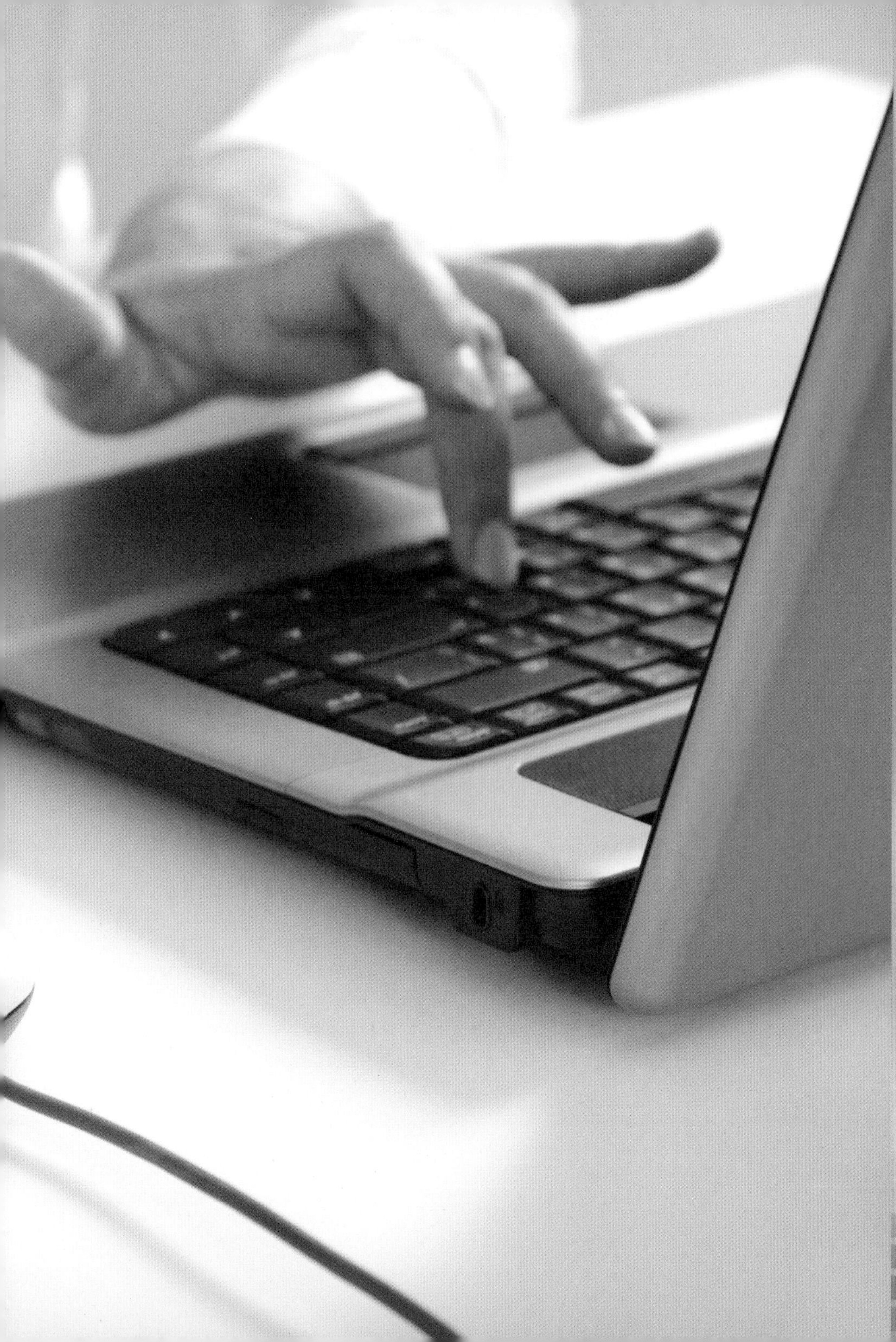

ALL ABOUT OFFICE

CHOOSE YOUR VERSION

Microsoft Office Suite is a collection of applications for doing office-type tasks. Among them are Word for word processing, Excel for spreadsheets, PowerPoint for presentations and Outlook for email. Different editions let you use Office on your computer, online or on your tablet or smartphone.

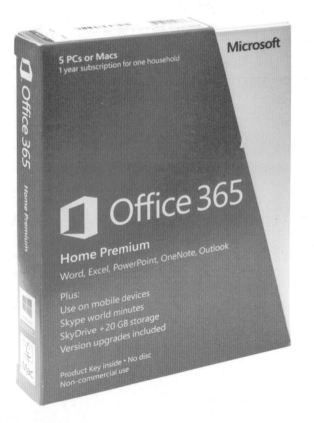

OFFICE 365

This is a subscription service that lets you use Office programs virtually anytime, anywhere and on any device. The latest versions of Office (Office 2013 for the PC or Office 2011 for the Mac) are available to download to your computer or use online.

Office 365 Programs

Your subscription entitles you to install fully working versions of:

○ **Word:** A word-processing program that lets you create, edit and print documents such as letters, reports and the like.

○ **Excel:** Creates spreadsheets to do your sums for everything from the household budget to a mortgage loan.

- **PowerPoint**: Helps you get your message across with dazzling slide presentations.

- **Outlook**: Your personal organizer, which handles your email, manages your contacts and has a calendar for scheduling your activities. Mac users can only sync with Microsoft Exchange-based email accounts.

- **OneNote**: The place to store your notes, web clippings and organize your ideas. Mac users have to download OneNote from the App Store.

Above: Different versions of Office let you work on your files from your desktop, the web, tablet and smartphone.

- **Publisher (PC only)**: Create your own publications, from newsletters to posters.

- **Access (PC only)**: Set up and manage databases.

Office 365 Options

- **Office 365 Personal**: Lets you install the latest Office programs on a single computer (PC or Mac), tablet and smartphone for a monthly or annual subscription.

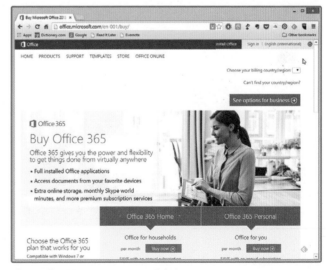

Above: Office 365 gives you access to all the latest programs.

○ **Office 365 Home:** Allows you to install the latest Office programs on up to five desktops or laptops (PC and Mac). In addition, you can use Office apps on up to five tablets, such as the Apple iPad or Microsoft Surface, and five smartphones.

> ## Hot Tip
>
> **All OneDrive accounts come with free storage space, currently 15 GB, while up to 1 Terabyte (TB) per user is available with Office 365 subscriptions.**

○ **Office 365 for Business:** Comes in different editions tailored to the size or type of business. In addition to the core Office applications there are options for:

- Exchange-based email: Hosted online.

- SharePoint: Lets businesses create websites to share documents and information.

Above: A subscription to Office 365 unlocks access to the Office programs as well as premium features on Office mobile apps.

- Lync, renamed Skype for Business: To contact others via instant messaging, video calls or online meetings.

ONEDRIVE – LINKING OFFICE BY THE CLOUD

With so many ways to work on your Office files, it could be a nightmare determining whether you have the latest version of the document, spreadsheet or presentation. To keep everything up to date, Office saves and stores your files in the cloud or, more precisely, OneDrive.

Sync Using OneDrive

From this storage space your files are automatically synced to any of your devices, so you can be sure you're always working with the latest version of a file. To sign up for your free OneDrive account, go to www.onedrive.com.

Accessing OneDrive

You can access and browse your OneDrive files using the different programs available for Windows and Mac computers, as well as separate apps for Android tablets and smartphones, iPads and iPhones, Windows Phones and even the Xbox.

Above: The free OneDrive account provides 15 GB of online storage for your Office files.

Above: The OneDrive tile for Windows 8.1 is just one way of accessing your online storage centre.

Automatically Saving to OneDrive

On PCs running Windows 8.1 you can select OneDrive as the default location for saving any Office files you create. To set it up:

○ Swipe in from the right of the screen, tap Settings then Change PC settings.

○ Alternatively, with the mouse, point to the lower-right corner, move the mouse pointer up to click Settings then Change PC settings.

○ Click or tap OneDrive, then select File storage and turn on Save documents to OneDrive by default.

Above: PCs running Windows 8.1 can save your files to OneDrive by default.

BUY OFFICE

If you prefer, you can opt to get Office the traditional way, as a one-time purchase. There are specific Office packages with different applications bundled together, or you can buy the individual programs separately.

One-time Purchase

The packages available are:

Above: Individual programs, like PowerPoint, can be bought in standalone versions.

- **Office Home & Student 2013**: Word, Excel, PowerPoint, OneNote on one PC.

- **Office Home & Business 2013**: Word, Excel, PowerPoint, OneNote, Outlook on one PC.

- **Office Professional 2013**: Word, Excel, PowerPoint, OneNote, Outlook, Publisher, Access on one PC.

- In addition, **standalone versions** are available for each of the individual Office applications.

- Mac users can buy **Office for Mac Home & Student** or **Office for Mac Home & Business**. These suites include Office 2011 applications (which is the latest version for the Mac).

Above: The most complete one-time purchase package is Office Professional 2013.

MOBILE OFFICE

Just because you're away from your PC, you don't have to stop work. You can still access your Office files, wherever you are, using apps that run on most tablets and smartphones, or through the browser on any PC or mobile device.

USING OFFICE ON YOUR TABLET

The lightweight nature of most tablets makes them ideal for working with your Office files on the go, particularly as the apps available will have most, if not all, of the features of the desktop versions.

Windows Tablets

These run the same version of Office 2013 applications as you have on your desktop. The only difference is that the buttons on the Ribbon are slightly larger and more spaced out for easier clicking by fingertip rather than mouse pointer.

iPad

There are custom-made mobile versions of several Office apps for the iPad:

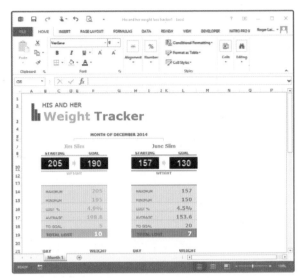

Above: This is the Excel Ribbon optimized for touch with more space between the commands.

- ○ **Separate Word, Excel and PowerPoint apps:** Let you view, create, edit and print files for free, if you sign in using your Microsoft account. There are also several premium features in each app, such as tracking and reviewing changes in Word, or adding and modifying chart elements in Excel, which are only available with an Office 365 subscription.

- ○ **OneNote app:** So you can take your digital notes with you.

- ○ **OWA for iPad:** Lets business users manage work emails, calendar, contacts and more in much the same way as the Outlook Web App does through the browser.

Above: You can also access Office online through the browser of your mobile device – here the iPad.

Differences with Desktop Versions

While the Office for iPad apps are similar to their desktop versions, there are noticeable differences:

- Although each app has a **Ribbon**, like the desktop version, it looks more like a **traditional toolbar**.

- The cut-down version of the Ribbon has **fewer tabs** but typically includes Home, Insert, Review and View.

- Tap an **icon** on the Ribbon and a drop-down menu will then open with various options.

- While the Office for iPad apps don't have the full range of features available in the desktop versions, they have the **essentials** to let you do most things you want with your files.

Above: Carry on working on a document you started on the desktop or online on your iPad.

Right: The Ribbon on programs like PowerPoint for the iPad looks more like a traditional toolbar.

OFFICE FOR SMARTPHONES

Previously, there was one Office Mobile app for smartphones that let you work on Word documents, Excel spreadsheets and PowerPoint presentations, synced with your OneDrive.

This Office hub is gradually being retired, starting with the iPad and iPhone, to be replaced with individual mobile apps for Word, Excel and PowerPoint (in the same way as OneNote, which has always been a separate app).

Hot Tip

Microsoft is launching Office apps for Android tablets, like the Samsung Galaxy Note, for the first time. Previously users had to go with third-party apps.

Above: Instead of one Office app there are now separate apps for the main programs.

Getting Started with Office Mobile Apps

○ From your phone you can **view**, **create** and **edit** your Office documents for free, although certain premium features aren't available unless you have an Office 365 subscription.

○ As content and formatting are kept intact, your documents will **look the same** on your smartphone as on your desktop and vice versa.

○ The new standalone Office apps have been specially designed for using on a phone, including a **vertical** version of the **Ribbon** and special views not available on the desktop:

Above: Your files look the same on your phone as the desktop.

- **Word**: Reflow view wraps content to your screen, so you don't have to pan.

- **Excel**: Has a full-screen view so you can just see the data.

- **PowerPoint**: Slideshow view lets you draw on slides as you're presenting.

○ Office apps now also connect with the online storage site **Dropbox**, so you can access, edit and share your Dropbox files from within the apps.

Above: There's a special vertical Ribbon for the Office phone apps.

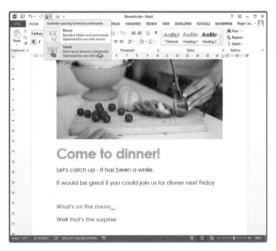

Above: You can extend the space between commands to make it touch-friendly and easier to use on a tablet.

OFFICE BY TOUCH

Some features in Office apps are designed to work specifically with touchscreens.

Touch Gestures

You can use typical touchscreen gestures – including tap, pinch, stretch, slide and swipe – to zoom into documents or move between pages.

On Windows tablets, which run the full desktop version of Office, or PCs with touchscreens, go to the Quick Access Toolbar, click the arrow beside the hand icon and select Touch. This spreads out the Command icons on the Ribbon so they're easier to use.

Below is a list of some of the most common touch gestures you are likely to use, complete with diagram.

Single-touch Gestures
Tap once: Equivalent to left-clicking with the mouse; use it to open an app, follow a link or similar.

Press and hold: Press down and leave your finger there for a moment. This is equivalent to right-clicking with the mouse to open a pop-up menu or get more information.

Slide: Dragging your finger across the screen is similar to clicking and holding with the mouse. It lets you pan or scroll through a list or web pages.

Swipe: Move your finger from the edge of the screen inwards, towards the centre.

Multi-touch Gestures
Pinch: Touch the screen with two fingers and move them together to zoom in or apart to zoom out.

Read Mode

This opens your documents in reading view, which minimizes distractions on screen by closing the Ribbon and toolbars, leaving most of the screen to display your text.

Zoom In

Double-tap with your finger (or double-click with the mouse) and you can make objects in your documents – such as tables or pictures – fill the screen. Tap away from the object and it goes back to normal size.

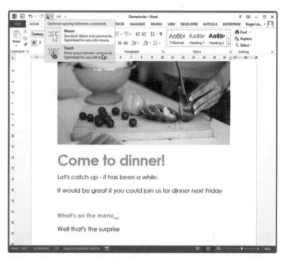

Above: You can extend the space between commands to make it touch-friendly and easier to use on a tablet.

OFFICE ONLINE

You can create or make changes to your Office files using cut-down, online versions of Office applications. These web apps work in your browser – they can't be downloaded to your PC, Mac or mobile device – so you can only use them when connected to the Internet.

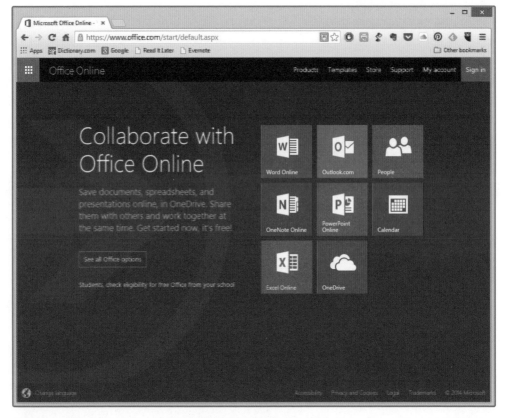

Above: Office Online lets you work on your Office files through your web browser.

STEP-BY-STEP: CREATING AND EDITING OFFICE FILES FOR FREE

1. To get started go to **Office.com**. You will need to sign in with your Microsoft account. Normally you will have one if you use other Microsoft services, such as Hotmail, or you may have an Outlook 365 account through work. There's also an option to sign up for a new account.

Above: While working in one Office web app, you can swap to another through the list of online services.

2. Select which Office web app you want to use. Here it's **Word**.

3. **Let's get started** offers you the choice of creating a new blank document, browsing the templates or accessing a Word document you already have stored on OneDrive, Microsoft's file storage service.

4. The Ribbon interface has fewer commands than the desktop version. But you can start your document online and then click

Above: To get started with Office Online you need to sign in with your Microsoft account.

the **Open In Word** to send the document to your desktop version of Word and carry on where you left off.

5. As you write, Word saves your changes automatically to OneDrive. You'll see **Saving**... or **Saved** in the status bar at the bottom.

> ## Hot Tip
>
> **Office Online files are automatically saved to OneDrive, which you can sync to your Mac or PC to view the documents offline.**

6. Alternatively, if you want to **edit** an Office file, go to OneDrive (click the downward-pointing arrow beside the service you're using and select the OneDrive icon) and navigate to the file you want. **Double-click** the file and it will automatically open in the correct Office Online app.

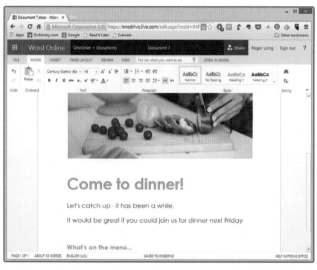

Above: On the Status bar you can see that Word Online has automatically saved the document to OneDrive.

7. It opens in View mode. To edit the file you'll need to be in **Editing view**. For Word documents, click Edit Document in the Ribbon then Edit in Word Online. It will be Excel or PowerPoint Online for a spreadsheet or presentation.

8. Once in **Edit mode** you can add or change text and pictures in Word, add functions or charts and sort data in Excel, or alter the graphics or notes of your presentation in PowerPoint.

Above: The Ribbon has fewer commands than other Word apps but you can send your document to the desktop version by clicking Open In Word.

Online Collaboration

Using Office Online you can invite friends and family to work on your documents, presentations, spreadsheets and notebooks at the same time. Just press the Share button at the top of the page. Invite people lets you email a link to a contact that will allow them to view or edit that version of the document. You can also choose whether or not they must have a Microsoft

account to access your file. Get a Link provides a URL for the file that you can send to people or put on your web page or blog. You can also choose whether to limit them to just viewing or editing your document.

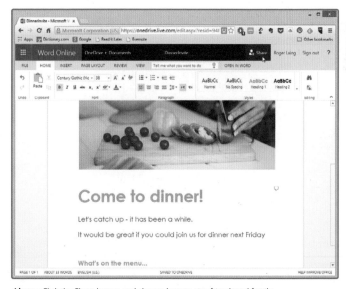

Adding Comments

The easiest way to show changes on shared documents is through comments:

1. **Select** the text you want to comment on.

Above: Click the Share button and choose how to give friends and family access to your document.

2. Click the Review tab and select **New Comment**.

3. Write in your idea, which will appear in the **Comments sidebar**.

4. Here, you can also see **other people's comments**.

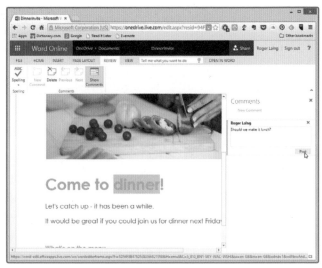

Above: Add your ideas to a shared document through the Comments sidebar.

Hot Tip

Switch between Office web apps as you work. Simply click the square mosaic in the left-hand corner beside the program name and select the service you want.

SHARING OFFICE FILES ONLINE

Having worked hard on your document, presentation or other content, you'll want to share it with others and display it in the best way possible. Using the web apps in Office Online there are various ways in which to share your work.

Display Office Files Directly on the Page

Rather than have a link on your blog or web page to download a file, it has more impact if it can be seen immediately on the page. This is known as embedding. You could, for example, show a PowerPoint presentation of your holiday cottage to rent, or your travel photos; you could add a discount voucher in Word, embed an Excel spreadsheet with a sales calculator, and so on.

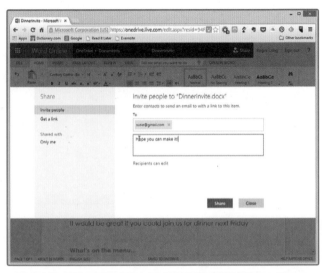

Above: Click Invite people to email a link to those with whom you want to share your online document.

Viewing Your Office Documents Online

Although you have created a document or presentation in Office, other people can still see it even if they don't have the program. At Office.com you can create a URL for the document, which you can then email to people or add to a page on your website or blog. When the link is clicked, Office Online runs in the browser. It means the viewer sees your Word document with the layout preserved, your Excel workbook has the data correctly filtered and sorted, and the animations work as intended in PowerPoint presentations.

Hot Tip

You can choose whether people you share the link with can view your document or edit it, or make it accessible to all by selecting Public.

Add Excel Interactive View

This adds a button to your table of information that lets people filter or sort the information in different ways. You can, for example, have a list of your top 10 ski resorts and the different costs associated with ski passes, accommodation, travel and so on. Excel Interactive View lets visitors to your web page filter the information according to what most interests them, for example the cost of skiing lessons.

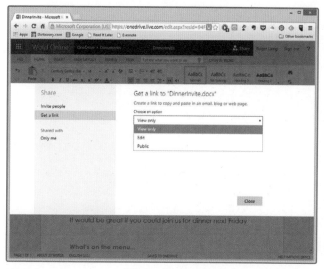

Above: Get a link lets you choose how freely to share access to your document.

WORD PROCESSING WITH WORD

WORD

Microsoft Word is word-processing software that lets you create professional-looking documents – from letters and reports to newsletters and flyers – virtually anywhere with versions of the program available for PC and Mac computers, tablet and smartphone.

WHAT IS WORD?

Word is like a digital typewriter but with many more features that save you time and avoid mistakes. Above all, it is What You See Is What You Get (WYSIWYG) as the layout you see on screen will be exactly the same when printed.

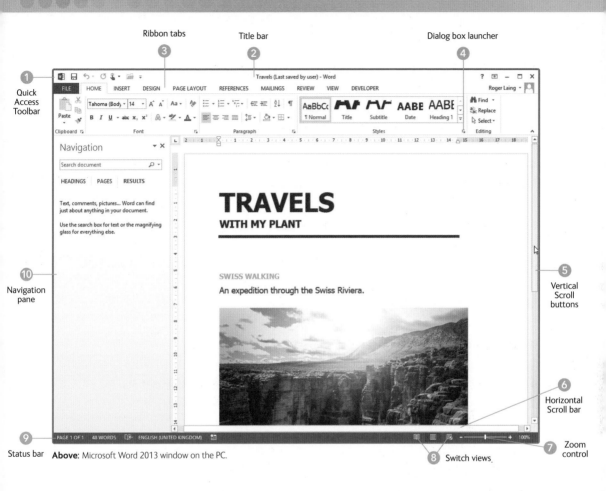

Ribbon tabs   Title bar   Dialog box launcher

Quick Access Toolbar

Navigation pane

Vertical Scroll buttons

Horizontal Scroll bar

Zoom control

Status bar   **Above:** Microsoft Word 2013 window on the PC.   Switch views

Word 2013 Window

1 **Quick Access Toolbar:** Commonly used commands here are always visible – such as Open, Save, Undo and Quick Print. More can be added and removed by clicking the drop-down arrow.

2 **Title bar:** This displays the name of the current document.

Hot Tip

The Ribbon can be minimized by double-clicking the tab name. Double-click again to restore it.

③ Ribbon tabs: Click on each one to see various Word buttons and commands that are grouped together into logically similar tasks:

- ○ **File**: Open, Save, Print and manage your Word files.

- ○ **Home**: The main tab that shows when Word opens has actions for changing fonts, formatting paragraphs, adding styles and more.

- ○ **Insert**: Lets you add tables, illustrations and other media.

- ○ **Design**: Alters the document formatting and background.

- ○ **Page Layout**: For setting up the page and paragraphs.

- ○ **References**: For handling longer documents.

- ○ **Mailings**: For adding special fields when using Word documents in mailshots.

- ○ **Review**: For proofing your documents and handling comments.

- ○ **View**: For changing the way you look at the document.

④ Dialog box launcher: Click this icon, positioned underneath a group of commands, to open a box with more options.

⑤ Vertical scroll buttons: Scroll up and down a document.

⑥ Horizontal scroll bar: Move left and right to scroll across the screen.

⑦ Zoom control: Drag the slider left or right to zoom in and out of the document.

8 **Switch views**: Change between Read View, Print View or Web View.

9 **Status bar**: Displays the number of pages and total number of words. If only some text is selected, it displays the word count of that selection.

10 **Navigation pane**: Press Ctrl+F to show. Reorganize long documents here by dragging the headings into a different position.

Word on the Mac

The latest standalone version for Apple Mac computers is Word 2011, but as shown here the layout is similar.

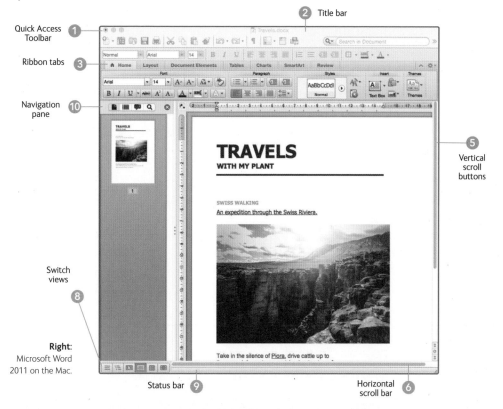

Right: Microsoft Word 2011 on the Mac.

GETTING STARTED WITH WORD

The finished output for anything you create in Word – whether it's a letter, report or poster – is called a document. With templates – in effect pre-formatted documents – Word provides a quick and easy way to get going.

USING WORD

The template features the fonts, styles, layout and other features that give the document its own look and feel.

Create a New Document

1. Go to the **File tab** on the Ribbon and choose **New** from the menu on the left. This opens the New window.

2. Select one of the featured **templates**, and in the window that opens click the **Create** button.

3. Other templates are available online; just enter a keyword for the sort of template you want in the Search box and click **Start Searching**.

Left: Pick a template or open a new blank document.

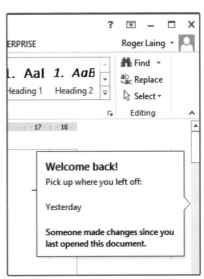

Hot Tip

The Resume Reading box appears when you reopen a Word document. A marker shows the page you last read and when you last viewed it.

Welcome back!
Pick up where you left off:

Yesterday

Someone made changes since you last opened this document.

Above: Word keeps tabs on how long you've been away and warns if anyone else has worked on your document.

4. Alternatively, choose the **Blank document** template to start from scratch. You can also press **Ctrl+N** on the keyboard to open a new document without opening the New window.

Open an Existing Document

Click the File tab, then Open and select a recent file from the list to reopen it. You can also press Ctrl+O (the letter, not the zero) for the Open dialog box to appear.

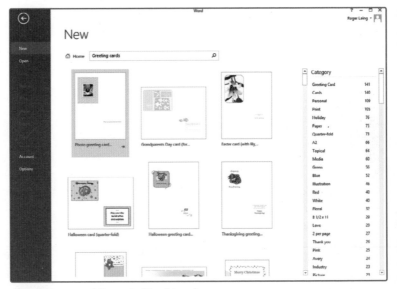

Above: You can search thousands of templates online.

Above: The Open dialog box lets you browse to where your Word documents are stored.

Above: Press Ctrl+S to open the Save As page.

Open a Copy of a Document

1. Click the **File tab**, select **Open** and choose the Word document to copy.

2. **Right-click** on the file.

3. Select **Open as Copy** from the pop-up menu.

4. The original is left intact and a **copy** of the document opens.

Saving a Document

If it's a new Word document, the quickest way is to press Ctrl+S to open the Save As page. Enter a name for the document and choose where to save it.

For existing documents, you can also press Ctrl+S or the Save button, which looks like a floppy disk, on the Quick Access Toolbar.

AutoSave Your Documents

Word takes responsibility for saving your work. Go to the File tab, select Options then Save. Here you can choose the time interval between saves and a default location for the saved Word documents.

CHANGING THE VIEW

There are times when you want to concentrate on different things in your document – such as the layout for printing or the text for proofing. Word makes this easier by having different views for your pages.

Views

You can move between Views using the Views button on the Status bar or selecting the relevant button on the View tab:

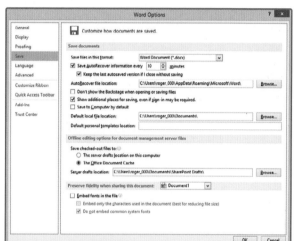

Above: The Word Options dialog box lets you set how often AutoSave saves your documents.

- **Read Mode:** The text fills as much of the screen as possible. To switch it off, click Close in the top-right corner.

- **Print Layout:** See how the text, graphics and margins in your document will appear when printed.

- **Web Layout:** Shows what your Word document would look like as a web page.

- **Outline:** Lists only the headings, so you can see the overall organization of your document.

- **Draft:** Margins are hidden to show more of the text, and page divisions are marked by faint dotted lines.

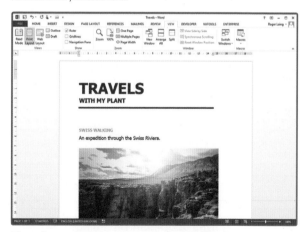

Above: You can change how you see your document from the View tab or Status bar.

WORKING WITH WORD

Once you've entered your text and images in Word your work is just starting. There are various ways you can alter the way the different elements on your page look to create some stunning documents.

TYPING AND FORMATTING TEXT

While most text you enter uses standard settings, there are some quick ways to change these as well as many others if you have the time.

Changing Your Default Settings

Each Word document has a number of settings for standard text (known as Normal) that cover the font, colour, size and other attributes:

1. To change this, open the Font dialog box by pressing **Ctrl+D**.

2. Go through and change any **settings** you wish.

3. Click the button labelled **Set As Default**.

4. A dialog box opens asking whether you want these settings to apply just to **this document** or to **all** those using the Normal settings.

Above: The Font dialog box lets you change the default settings for your text.

Changing Parts of Your Document

To change the settings for individual sections of text, highlight the text and then use the buttons and commands on the Home tab to change font, size and so on.

Adding Bold, Underline and Italics

These can be changed using the Formatting toolbar on the Ribbon's Home tab or the following shortcuts:

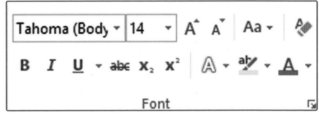

- ○ **Bold**: Ctrl+B.
- ○ **Underline**: Ctrl+U.
- ○ **Italics**: Ctrl+I.
- ○ **Double underline**: Ctrl+Shift+D.

Above: Change the appearance of your text from the Font group.

Changing Font Size with the Keyboard

Select the text you want to change: to increase the size, press Ctrl+Shift+ the > key; to make it smaller, press Ctrl+Shift+ the < key.

Changing Alignment

Select the text and use the buttons in the Paragraph group on the Home tab or the following shortcut keys:

- ○ **Left align a paragraph**: Ctrl+L.
- ○ **Right align a paragraph**: Ctrl+R.
- ○ **Centre a paragraph**: Ctrl+E.
- ○ **Left and right justify a paragraph**: Ctrl+J.

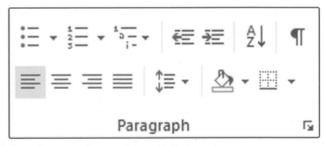

Press the keys again to switch back to left aligned.

Above: Change the alignment of your text in the Paragraph group.

Alter Line Spacing

To avoid text looking too cramped you might have to vary the spacing between each line of text. The quickest way is to select the content affected and apply the following shortcut keys:

- ○ **Single**: Ctrl+1.
- ○ **Double**: Ctrl+2.
- ○ **1.5 lines**: Ctrl+5.

AutoFormat

Word can save you time by automatically formatting your text as you type:

1. To change the options available go to the File tab, select Options, then Proofing and in the dialog box that opens, click **AutoCorrect Options** and select the **AutoFormat** tab.

2. Select the **options** you want, such as converting a website address to a clickable link, replacing hyphens with a dash and correctly displaying fractions.

Right: AutoFormat will format your text as you type.

> ## Hot Tip
>
> **If too many different and conflicting formats are applied, turn back the changes and apply the default settings by selecting the text and pressing the Ctrl key and space bar.**

AutoText

Instead of repeatedly typing the same phrases – such as a letter sign-off – Word can store them and apply them automatically:

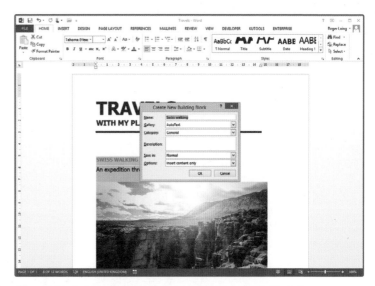

Above: Rather than type the same phrases over and over, use Autotext to do it for you.

- **To create an AutoText entry:** Select the text to use, press Alt+F3 on the keyboard and the Create New Building Block dialog box appears to create the entry. Fill in the information and click OK.

- **To apply an AutoText entry:** Click the Insert tab, then Quick Parts and AutoText. Click the entry to add it.

WORKING WITH IMAGES

Add some visual colour to your documents with images that you can source from your computer or online.

Adding Images

The main ways to add images are:

- **From your computer:** Click where you want your image to go, then on the Insert tab select the Pictures button. In the dialog box that opens, browse to where your images are saved on the computer, select the image to use and then press the Open button.

Above: Enter a keyword to search for pictures online.

○ **From online:** Select the Online Pictures button from the Insert tab. In the dialog box that opens enter a keyword that describes the image you want. You can search Office.com, which includes Microsoft's library of free clip art, Bing or your OneDrive account. Select the picture you want and click the Insert button.

Aligning Images and Text

You can change the way text wraps around images that are added. Right-click inside the image and select Wrap Text, then choose your preferred option:

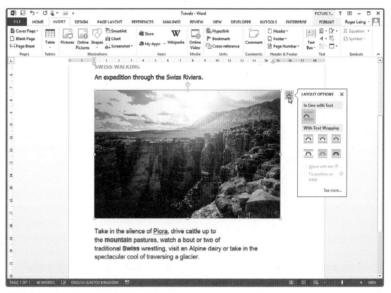

Above: Layout options lets you change the way text wraps round a picture.

- **Square**: Text goes round the border of the image.

- **Tight**: Wraps the text close to the image.

- **Behind Text**: Runs the text over the image.

- **Top and Bottom**: Puts the image on its own line. This is the default setting.

Cropping Your Image

To use only part of an image or trim off unwanted bits, you can crop the picture:

- Select the image and the **Picture Tools Format tab** appears.

- Click the **Crop button** and choose the appropriate option.

Hot Tip

Another good indication of how your document will look when printed is the Print Layout view, accessed via the View tab.

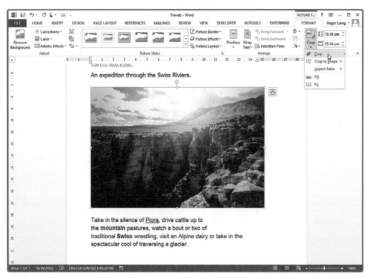

Above: The Crop tool lets you trim or reshape your image.

○ **Crop:** Allows manual cropping.

○ **Crop to shape:** Allows the image to be changed to a shape, such as a round box, circle or heart.

○ **Aspect ratio:** Provides a list of pre-set ratios for width and height (most photographs use an aspect ratio of 3:2).

Above: Print Layout view shows how your document will look when printed.

PRINTING

Having got your document the way you want it, you'll want to share it. Often that involves printing out your document in its full glory. Before you do though, there are a few things to check.

Print Preview

The best check for how your document will print out is Print Preview:

- To access it, click the **File tab** and then **Print** in the menu on the left-hand side.

- An even quicker way to get to the Print Preview screen is to press **Ctrl+F2**.

Changing Printing Settings

Print Preview allows you to change various settings:

- **Print All Pages**: To print all or to choose which pages to print.

- **Orientation**: Either portrait or landscape.

- **Size**: Typically letter or A4.

- **Margins**: Change these to alter the amount of white space around your document.

- **Page Per Sheet**: Lets you print several documents on a single piece of paper.

- **Printer**: Select the printer to use. Click on Printer Properties and there are printer-specific settings available, such as fitting the document on one page.

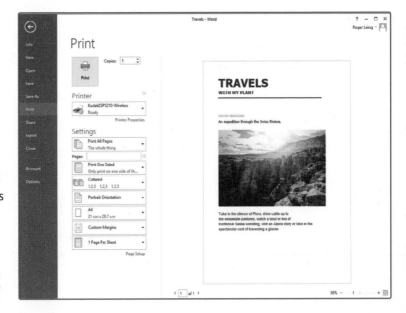

Right: Print Preview is on the right with the boxes to change the settings on the left.

WORD ON THE GO

When you are out and about you can still access your Word files. There are mobile apps for creating and editing Word documents or web apps for working on your files online.

MOBILE WORD

Although the Word apps for smartphones and tablets generally have fewer features than the desktop version, they enable you to do most tasks.

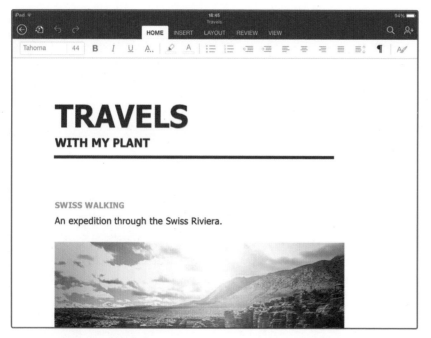

Tablets and Smartphones

Microsoft will be replacing its single mobile app for all Office in favour of a standalone Word app for Windows, iOS and Android devices. The app lets you view, create and edit Word documents, although it does require a Microsoft account.

Above: The iPad Word app has fewer commands but it can create documents and do most essential editing tasks.

Hot Tip

There are premium features in the Word app only available with an Office 365 account. These include putting your text in columns and advanced editing capabilities.

Word Online

- The **Word web app** is part of Office Online.

- Signing-in through your free **Microsoft account** you can work for free on your documents through a browser on any PC or mobile device.

Above: The commands in the Word app scroll vertically.

- Although the web app has limited features, it does include most **formatting** commands and allows you to change **page layouts**.

- Files you work on are automatically saved to **OneDrive**.

- You can invite others to **share** your documents and add comments.

Right: The Word web app lets you change the layout of your page.

	zł	$	$
	338,98 zł	$2,20	
	342,75 zł	$2,20	
	369,03 zł	$2,21	
	379,18 zł	$2,21	$
	384,75 zł	$2,21	$
	404,35 zł	$2,21	$
	414,87 zł	$2,21	$1
	415,60 zł	$2,21	$13
	417,77 zł	$2,21	$140
	425,02 zł	$2,21	$143
	433,00 zł	$2,21	$145,3
	445,70 zł	$2,22	$147,5
	456,72 zł	$2,22	$149,79
	465,42 zł	$2,22	$152,00
	466,87 zł	$2,22	$154,22
	466,87 zł	$2,22	156,445669
	479,57 zł	$2,22	$158,67
	499,15 zł	$2,22	$160,89
	510,02 zł	$2,22	$16
	522,52 zł	$2,23	
	543,96 zł	$2,23	

123,27	57	509,02		
125,47	58	514,36		
27,67	59	519,66		
9,88	60	524,932		
2,09	61	530,164		
29	62	535,362		
0	63	540,526		
1	64	545,658		
	65	550,758		
	66	555,826		
	67	560,864		
	68	565,872		
69	69	570,85		
70	70	575,8		
71	71	580,721		
2		585,6		

EXCEL FOR SPREADSHEETS

EXCEL

As well as doing calculations, Excel is a good place to store your data. Put the two together and you have the ideal program to track your personal finances, compare prices, list your valuables and much more.

WHAT IS EXCEL?

Excel is a spreadsheet program where you can store, organize and work on data. The data – or information you put in – is shown on a rectangular grid made up of rows and columns.

Excel's Jargon

- **Spreadsheet**: The generic name for the files created by Excel.

- **Worksheet**: The single page or sheet within the spreadsheet itself. Each worksheet is shown as a tab at the bottom of the page.

- **Workbook**: Microsoft's name for an Excel file that contains one or more worksheets.

- **Rows**: The line of cells down a spreadsheet. Each row has a number displayed on the left of the worksheet. Each worksheet can have over 1,048,576 rows.

- **Columns**: The cells across a spreadsheet. Each column is identified by a letter, starting A to Z, then AA to AZ, and so on. A single worksheet can have 16,384 columns.

- **Cells**: A particular point in the spreadsheet marked by a cell address, for example, A1 refers to column A and row number 1.

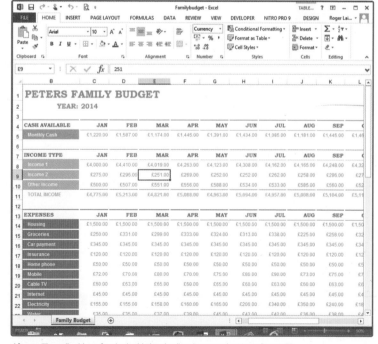

Above: The cell address for the highlighted cell is shown in the Name Box as E9.

Excel 2013 Window

① **Quick Access Toolbar**: Visible, even if you hide the Ribbon, it has some buttons for regular tasks like Open, Save, Undo and Print.

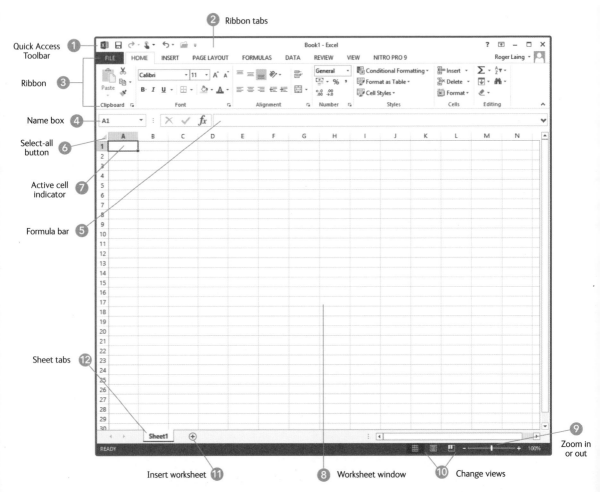

Above: Microsoft Excel 2013 on the PC.

2 **Ribbon tabs**: These are context-sensitive, so when you click a tab the available buttons and commands change. The tabs are labelled:

- **File**: Lets you open, save, print and share files.

- **Home**: This has the main commands for inserting, editing and formatting data.

- **Insert**: Here you can add tables, charts and the like to illustrate your data.

- **Page Layout**: Set page margins, breaks and print areas.

- **Formulas**: Select the functions to use on your data or troubleshoot formulas.

- **Data**: Import your data then sort, filter and analyze it.

- **Review**: Proof your file and add comments.

- **View**: Change the way you view your workbook.

3 **Ribbon**: Underneath each tab is a set of related commands, grouped into similar actions, for example, Charts on the Insert tab.

4 **Name box**: This has the address of the currently selected cell.

5 **Formula bar**: Enter or edit the content in the selected cell. (For a list of Excel formulas, plus tips and tricks on how to use them, visit www.ozgrid.com/Excel.)

6 **Select-all button**: Selects the entire worksheet.

7 **Active cell indicator**: Shown by a dark border around the cell(s).

⑧ Worksheet window: The grid with your content. Right-click the cells to open a box with the commands relevant to your data.

⑨ Zoom in or out: Use the slider control.

⑩ Change views: Select between Normal, Page Layout or Page Break Preview.

⑪ Insert worksheet: Click the + button to add a new worksheet.

⑫ Sheet tabs: These display the names of the worksheets. Click a tab to make it active.

Hot Tip

To see more of your worksheet at the same time, split the window. Select the row or column where you want the divide, click the View tab and press Split.

Excel on the Mac

The latest standalone version for Apple Mac computers is Excel 2011. Although it has a different look to the PC version, most of the features are the same.

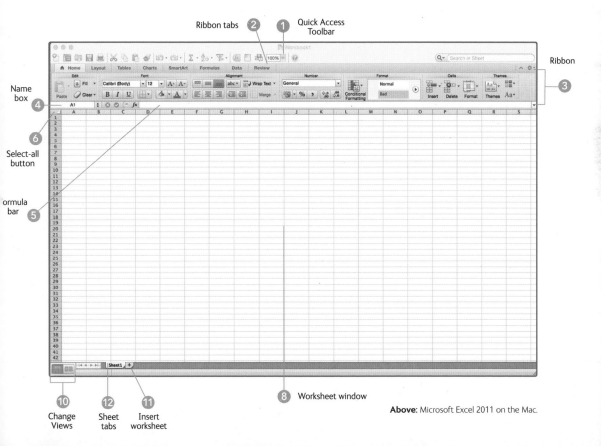

Above: Microsoft Excel 2011 on the Mac.

GETTING STARTED WITH EXCEL

Excel is a great tool for helping you get valuable information out of a lot of data. It works as well for simple calculations as it does for tracking information.

USING EXCEL

At the heart of Excel is the grid of cells, which can contain numbers, text or formulas that can then be added up, sorted, filtered and even shown in charts.

Create a New Workbook

Go to the File tab on the Ribbon and choose New to open the New window.

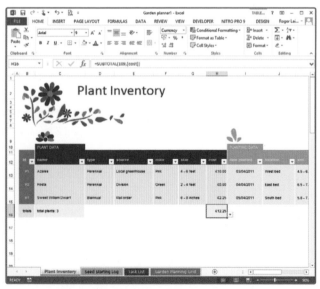

Above: The flexibility of Excel is shown by the variety of data it can hold.

- ○ **Choose a template:** A pre-formatted workbook with a specific purpose, such as budgeting or running an inventory. Select one and click the Create button.

- ○ **Search online:** You can source other templates by entering a keyword in the Search box, then clicking on Start Searching.

- ○ **To start from scratch:** Choose the Blank document template.

Above: There are many templates to choose from.

Open an Existing Workbook

Click the File tab, then Open and select a recent file from the list, or press Ctrl+O to access the Open dialog box.

Saving a Workbook

When saving a new Excel spreadsheet, press Ctrl+S and enter a name and location in the Save As dialog box.

In existing workbooks, press Ctrl+S or the Save button on the Quick Access Toolbar.

AutoSave Your Workbooks

Go to the File tab, select Options then Save. In the AutoRecover section select the time interval between saves and a default location for saving your workbooks.

Right: The Excel Options dialog box lets you choose how often Excel saves your workbooks.

WORKING WITH EXCEL

Excel is remarkably flexible in the ways it lets you add data to your worksheet. However, as the data can take a number of forms – numbers, dates, text or even times – you do have to make sure it appears in the right format.

ENTERING INFORMATION

It can be very monotonous to add rows and columns of figures and the like to a worksheet. Fortunately, there are shortcuts which let Excel do the hard work.

Adding Data to a Cell

- **Click the tick mark** next to the formula bar when you've finished typing or press Enter/Return on the keyboard.

- **Click the cross mark**: Similar to the Undo button this lets you revert to the cell's original contents.

- **Cancel editing a cell** by pressing the Escape key.

Above: Click the cross mark to go back to a cell's original content.

AutoComplete

- Excel helps you complete lists by offering **suggestions** based on previous entries.

- When list entries start with the **same letter** (for example 'gas bill' or 'groceries') Excel will offer suggestions as you enter more letters.

C4	▾	:	✕ ✓ *fx*	Supermarket		
	A	B	C	D	E	F
1	Date	Amount	Type of Expense			
2	03-Sep	£88.00	Supermarket			
3	08-Sep	£56.40	Petrol			
4	09-Sep	£102.00	Supermarket			
5						
6						
7						
8						

Above: When entering data, AutoComplete will suggest entries based on those above, provided none of these is blank.

- If there are any **blank cells** in a list, Excel will not check the entries above it.

Select Cells

- **Shift and click:** This is the easiest way to highlight a range of cells. Click the cell top left then move the mouse pointer to the bottom-right cell, press the Shift key and left-click.

- **Ctrl and click:** Press the Ctrl key and left-click inside individual cells, or a range of cells, to select them.

Cut, Copy and Paste

- **Cut:** Select the cells and press the Delete key. To cut content, ready to paste, press Ctrl+X.

- **Copy:** Press Ctrl+C and a moving dotted line appears around the selected cell(s).

Hot Tip

To ignore an AutoComplete entry, overwrite it by continuing to type, or press the Delete key.

- **Paste**: Once the data is cut or copied, select the destination cell (or the first cell in a range) and press Enter to paste the content. Alternatively, press Ctrl+V.

- **Cancel**: To stop the move, press Escape.

Smart Tags

When pasting your data into cells a Smart Tag appears bottom right. This has a variety of paste options that can fix issues such as incorrect formatting.

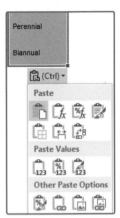

Above: When you paste data in a cell, the Smart Tag offers various paste options.

Deleting Cell Contents

- **To do this without changing the formatting**: Select the cells and press the Delete key.

- **To delete cell formatting**: Such as where a number has been changed to a date, select the cells, click the Home tab then the Clear button, and select Clear Formats from the pop-up menu.

Deleting Rows and Columns

Right-click the row number or column letter and choose Delete from the pop-up menu.

Left: The Clear button, which looks like an eraser, is in the Editing section of the Home tab.

Inserting Rows and Columns

Position the mouse pointer below the row or to the right of the column where you want to add the extra row or column. Right-click and choose Insert from the pop-up menu.

Editing Data

○ **Press F2**: A cursor appears inside the cell. Use the arrow keys, Delete and Backspace to make changes.

○ **Double-click inside the cell**: The flashing cursor appears ready for you to edit the contents.

○ **Use the Formula bar**: Select the cell and its contents will be displayed in the Formula bar, where you can make your edits.

CALCULATIONS

As a spreadsheet program, Excel is all about calculations, which can be as simple as adding up your expenses or as complex as working out depreciation rates on a loan.

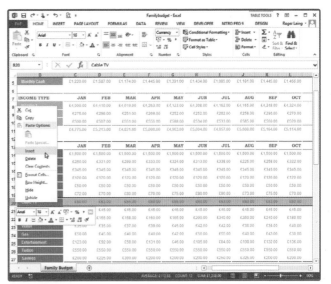

Above: To add an extra row, right-click on the row and select Insert from the pop-up menu.

Above: Enter data for the cell in the Formula bar.

Hot Tip

See the results of your calculations on the Status bar. Select a range of cells and the total, the average and a count will appear.

Follow the Rules

○ Always start a calculation with an equals (=) sign, otherwise Excel will show the text rather than the result of the calculation.

Above: As cell E1 is an absolute cell reference it can be used for many calculations. So to change the VAT rate to affect multiple calculations, you just need to alter it in one cell.

○ Use the standard symbols for calculations: so + for addition, - for subtraction, asterisk (*) for multiplication and forward slash (/) for division.

○ Include dollar signs next to the cell addresses to make it an 'absolute cell reference'. This will not change if copied elsewhere. This is useful, for example, when calculations all reference one particular cell, such as the VAT rate. If VAT changes, then only one cell has to change.

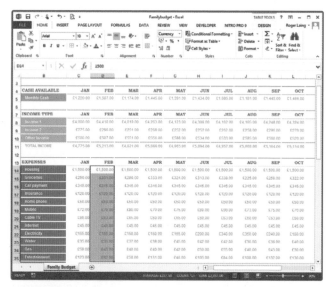

Above: Select a range of cells and the total, average and a count of the number of cells will be shown in the Status bar.

STEP-BY-STEP: BASIC CALCULATIONS WITH AUTOSUM

1. Select an **empty cell** at the bottom of a list of numbers, or to the right of them.

2. Go to the **Formulas tab** and click the **AutoSum button**, which has the Greek letter sigma (Σ) beside it.

3. Excel automatically creates an **=SUM** calculation showing the cell range.

4. If this is correct, press **Enter/ Return**.

5. If the cell references are incorrect, just select the correct ones to **overwrite** the calculation.

Other AutoSum Calculations

Once you've mastered the basic calculations, there are other calculations you can pick from the drop-down menu on the AutoSum button, including:

○ **Average:** The mean average value of the selected cells.

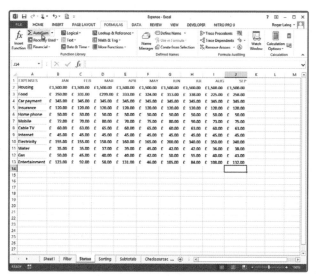

Above: Select an empty cell under the numbers you want to total and click AutoSum.

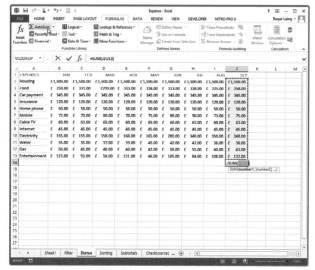

Above: If the range of cells is wrong you can adjust it before AutoSum does the calculation.

- **Count Numbers**: The number of cells containing numbers.

- **Max**: The highest number in a range of cells.

- **Min**: The lowest number in a range of cells.

STEP-BY-STEP: ADDING CHARTS

- Making a **chart** from your data makes it easier to spot trends.

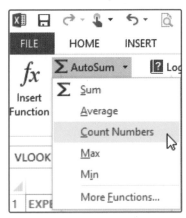

Above: AutoSum can perform a variety of calculations on the selected cells.

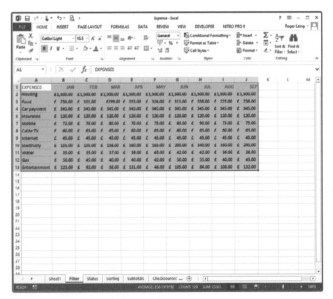

Above: It is best if the data for your chart is in a table with column or row labels.

- To create your chart, it's easier if your data is in a table with **column headings** or **row labels** (or both).

- **Select** the data to include (plus any headings or row labels) and press **F11**.

- The new chart will be displayed in a **separate worksheet**.

- To have it appear beside the selected cells, press **Alt+F1** instead.

- To **modify** the chart, click the chart area, right-click the chart and choose **Change Chart Type**.

○ In the dialog box that opens are the different chart types – **pie charts**, **line charts**, **scatter graphs** and so on – and styles such as **3D**.

Above: Press Alt+F1 to have the chart displayed beside the data on the same worksheet.

PRINTING

The exceptional size of some worksheets in Excel can make printing difficult. Fortunately, Excel has a few techniques to assist with the presentation of your printout.

Print Preview

○ Click the File tab and choose Print to open the **Print Preview** screen.

○ This shows how the printout will look and lets you change various **print settings**:

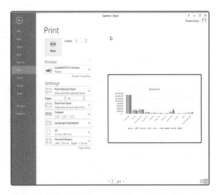

Above: Print Preview shows what the printout will look like, while allowing you to change print settings on the left.

- **Change orientation**: From landscape to portrait.

- **Shrink the printout**: Choose an option by clicking the Fit All Columns on One Page button.

- **Alter the margins**: Click the Margins button and increase or decrease the space around the page.

Above: Select Print Preview and Print from the drop-down menu to add it to the Quick Access Toolbar.

Hot Tip

Add Print Preview to the Quick Access Toolbar. Click the drop-down arrow beside the menu and select Print Preview and Print.

Set Print Area

It might be the case that you only want to print out a certain part of your worksheet. Rather than printing out the entire thing; you can set a specific print area. To set this up, simply follow these instructions:

1. **Select** the cells you want.

2. On the Page Layout tab click the Print Area button and select **Set Print Area**.

3. To go back and print the **whole worksheet**, follow the same process but select Clear Print Area.

Above: Rather than print the whole worksheet, the Print Area button lets you select an area to be printed.

MOBILE EXCEL

While most of the Excel apps for smartphones and tablets don't have all the features of the desktop version, you'll find that they have most of the essential capabilities.

Tablets and Smartphones

The standalone Excel app for Windows, iOS and Android devices lets you create and edit Excel spreadsheets for free.

There are premium features available with an Office 365 account, including advanced editing for text, pictures and charts.

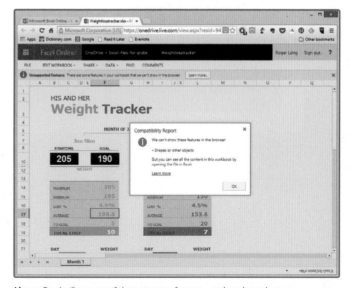

Above: Carry on with Excel on your iPad where you left off with Excel on your desktop.

Excel Online

○ Excel is part of Office Online, which allows you to work on your documents through a **browser** on any PC or mobile device.

○ Although the web app has limited features, it does include **data sorting** and **charts**.

○ Your files are automatically saved to your **OneDrive**.

Above: Excel will warn you if there are some features – such as shapes here – that aren't supported in the online version of the program.

GET ORGANIZED WITH OUTLOOK

OUTLOOK

Outlook is a desktop application for reading email, managing calendars and organizing your contacts. In addition, Outlook.com is a personal webmail service, similar to Gmail, which lets you access your mail online and through mobile devices.

WHAT IS OUTLOOK?

Outlook 2013 is the Office application you use to manage your communications – via email and social networks – as well as organize your time, the people you know and the activities you have planned.

Setting Up Outlook

The first thing to do before you can start to send and receive emails is to add your email account. Click the File tab then the Add Account button:

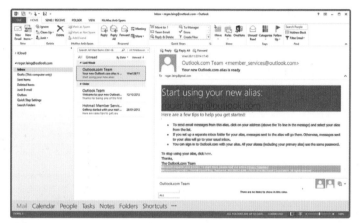

Above: Outlook is the desktop program that can link you to online email services, including Outlook.com.

- ◗ **Student or company accounts:** If your company, university or college uses Microsoft Exchange for its email, Outlook 2013 will try to set up the account for you.

- ◗ **Internet email accounts:** For accounts such as Hotmail, Outlook.com (see below), Gmail or Yahoo, simply enter your name, email address and password to get started.

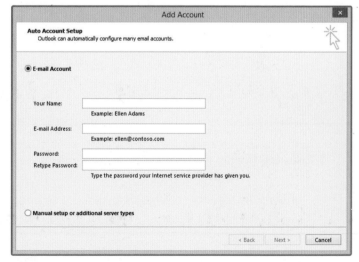

Above: Outlook does the hard work of connecting you to your email accounts. All it needs is your email address and password.

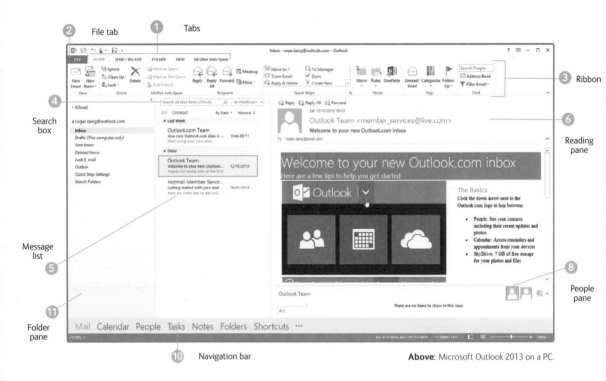

Above: Microsoft Outlook 2013 on a PC.

Outlook 2013 Window

1. **Tabs**: This is the view of the Home tab, which you will work in most of the time.

2. **File tab**: Use this to access the backstage view to add accounts and change settings.

3. **Ribbon**: This has all the commands for different actions grouped together into similar tasks. For example, the commands to Reply, Reply All or Forward an email are all in the Respond group.

4. **Search box**: Click the drop-down arrow to select where you want to search, which can range from the current mailbox to all Outlook items.

⑤ Message list: Scroll down the list to toggle on or off the flag that marks individual messages as important, mark them as read or unread, delete them and so on.

⑥ Reading pane: This can be set underneath or to the right of the messages or switched off completely from the option list beside the reading pane icon on the View tab. In Outlook 2013 you can reply to your emails direct from the reading pane.

⑦ To-Do bar: This has options to add a calendar, a list of your favourite people, contacts and your task list.

⑧ People pane: This has details on every name the message is addressed to, plus a list of recent emails from the same address.

⑨ Peek box: Hover over the different headings – like Calendar, People or Tasks – and get a quick view of what's happening.

⑩ Navigation bar: Select the different buttons to move between Mail, Calendar, People (your contacts), Tasks, Notes and so on.

⑪ Folder pane: This shows all your accounts and lists the different folders, or mailboxes, for each.

> ## Hot Tip
> You can have two or more folders, such as Calendar or Notes, open at the same time in separate windows. Simply right-click a folder or Navigation button and select Open in New Window.

Above: Opening individual folders in a new window lets you multitask, such as looking at an email and checking your calendar at the same time.

Outlook on the Mac

The latest standalone version for Apple Mac computers is Outlook 2011. Although it has a different look to the PC version, most of the features are the same.

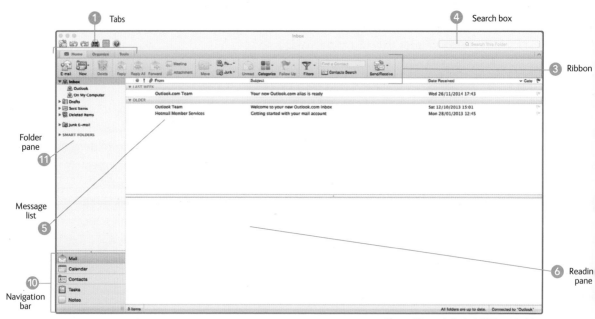

Above: Microsoft Outlook 2011 on the Mac.

Above: Link your contacts on social networks like Facebook and LinkedIn.

Social Networks

Outlook can connect to sites like Facebook or LinkedIn. Click the File tab, then the arrow beside Account Settings and select Social Network Accounts. Enter the login details for the account you want to use and click the Connect button.

HANDLING EMAIL

Outlook is mainly thought of as an application for managing emails, but it is also capable of handling many other tasks.

Send an Email

1. From any mail folder, click the **New Email button** to open a message window.

2. Enter the **name(s)** of the people you're sending it to in the To... text box.

3. Let them know what the email's about by adding a descriptive **subject line**.

4. **Type** your message. Check there are no embarrassing typos by clicking the **Spelling & Grammar** button on the Review tab.

5. Save a **draft**. If you're not ready to send or want to check something, click the Save button then close the message window and it will be saved in the Drafts folder. When you're ready, open this folder and double-click the message to continue writing.

6. Send when ready by clicking the **Send button** or pressing **Alt+S**.

Add an Email Address

Above: To send an email, start by clicking the New Email button.

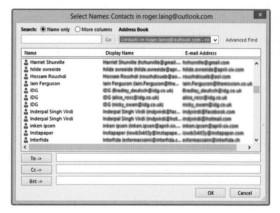

Above: Clicking the To... or Cc... button opens the contacts list for you to select the email addresses to add.

- **Use Outlook Contacts:** Click the To... or Cc... (carbon copy) button. Choose who you want from the Select Names dialog box that opens and add them to your email by pressing the To... button. Press the Cc... button for the email to be copied to the contact you include.

- **Manually enter an address**: If you know the address, type or paste it into the To... or Cc... fields.

- **Reply to a message**: Select the message in your mailbox, click the Reply button and the address is entered automatically. Click Reply All to include everyone who received the original message.

Add Attachments

1. In the email message window select the Insert tab then click the **Attach File** button.

2. **Browse** through the dialog box to locate and select the file you want to send.

3. **Ctrl+click** the filenames if there are several files to send.

4. Click **Insert** to add them to your email.

Add Photos

1. To send photos that are **embedded** in your email message, rather than as attachments, you have to use HTML format. Click the Format Text tab, then the **HTML button**.

Hot Tip

Select Bcc... for a blind carbon copy, which sends the email to an address you add but doesn't show the recipient's name in the same email received by the other people.

Above: Click the Attach File button on the Insert tab to add attachments to your message.

Above: For photos to appear inline – that is inside the message – you have to make sure the HTML button is set on the Format Text tab.

2. Click the **Insert tab**.

3. Click in the email where you want to **position** the photo, then the **Pictures** button.

4. **Locate** and select the photo you want, and press the **Insert** button to add it.

Forward a Message

1. Click the **Forward** button and the message opens with the text of the original email.

2. Add any text you want to the message and the addresses of those you're forwarding it to, then click the **Send** button.

3. Unlike replying to a message, when you forward an email any photos or files **attached** will also be sent.

Find That Mail

The Search box is your starting point for all searches. The results will appear as a list in the window below. To return to the full list of contents in a folder click the Close Search button (X).

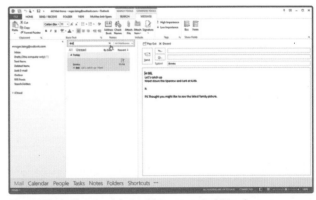

Above: Click the Close Search button (X) to return to the full list of your email messages.

CONTACTS

People is your contacts folder, the digital address book with all the information you need to keep in touch with friends and family, from email addresses to phone numbers and social network handles (names).

MANAGING YOUR CONTACTS

It can be difficult to keep up to date with the latest information on your contacts. Fortunately, Outlook makes it simple to add new contacts and by linking the program with social networks some information will be automatically updated.

Add a New Contact

○ **From a message:** Right-click on the sender's name in the From: line of the email and select Add to Outlook contacts from the menu.

○ **Keyboard shortcuts:** When in Contacts press Ctrl+N. In other folders use Ctrl+Shift+C.

○ **On the Home tab:** Click the New Contact button and add details to the contact form.

Contact Groups

If you regularly send messages to the same group of people – such as your Sunday football team – you can create one email address for them. When you send an email you simply use this one address rather than several.

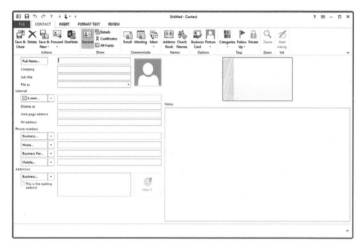

Above: Press the New Contact button to open the detailed contacts form.

STEP-BY-STEP: SET UP A CONTACT GROUP

1. Click the **People** button on the Navigation bar.

Above: You can add as much – or as little – information to your contacts through the People button in the Navigation bar.

Above: Click the New Contact Group button to start setting up a communal email address.

2. Go to the Home tab and click the **New Contact Group** button. Unfortunately this feature does not work with Exchange ActiveSync (EAS) accounts like Outlook.com or live.com. You'll know if you have an EAS account as the New Contact Group button will be greyed out.

3. In the box that opens add a **name** that describes the group – here it's SuperWhites.

4. Click the **Add Members** button.

5. If the names aren't already in your Contacts folder choose **New Email Contact** from the drop-down list.

6. More likely they will already be in your **Contacts** folder, so you can select From Outlook Contacts.

7. Hold down the **Ctrl key** as you select the names you want to include.

8. Click the **Members** button then OK, and the names are added to the Group. Click **Save and Close**.

Above: You can add members to the list from a variety of sources.

CALENDAR

Outlook's Calendar will help you manage your time, day by day, by scheduling appointments and events and letting you know where you have to be.

SETTING UP SCHEDULES

Outlook distinguishes between appointments – like a meeting with the bank manager at a certain time on a particular day – and events which tend to last all day, such as birthdays.

Add a New Appointment or Event

1. Select the **date(s)**.

2. On the Home tab click the **New Appointment** button.

3. The **Appointment tab** should have the date or dates you selected earlier. If not, change it and enter the subject, location and a start and end time.

Hot Tip

If your appointment clashes with another you've scheduled you'll get a warning alert. Click the Calendar button to look for available timeslots.

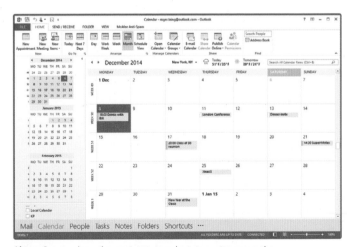

Above: See at a glance the appointments and events coming up over the next month.

> ## Hot Tip
>
> Click the Share Calendar icon on the Ribbon and you can send an email link to a friend to access your calendar.

4. Check the **All day event** box to make it an event.

5. To make it a repeating appointment or event, click the **Recurrence** button and set how often it recurs – for example weekly or yearly – and the end date, if any.

6. To be reminded just before the scheduled activity starts, click the **alarm bell** on the Ribbon and select the relevant time period.

Above: On the Appointment tab you can enter a start and end time.

Right: The Appointment Recurrence window lets you set how frequently to repeat the event as well as the end date, if any.

TASKS, REMINDERS AND NOTES

It's easy to forget the million and one things you have to do. So Outlook includes a Tasks window where you can list what has to be done and get reminders when things are due.

TASK MASTER

The Tasks window is your eye on what needs to be done, which things on your to-do list have been finished and those that are overdue.

Entering Tasks

Start writing in the Click here field to add a new Task box at the top of the Tasks reading pane. Enter the subject then press the Tab key to enter the date due and category of task.

Organizing Tasks

○ **Folder pane:** Under My Tasks you can choose:

- **To-Do List:** This includes all tasks, including those created from email messages or calendar appointments.

Above: To enter a task just start typing in the Click here field to add a new Task box.

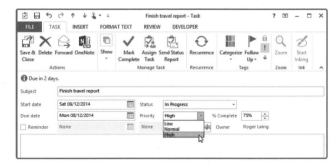

Above: A fuller range of task options – including setting the priority – is available through the full Task window.

Above: The commands in the Arrangement group on the View tab let you organize your task list according to different criteria.

- **Tasks:** This just shows the jobs you've set yourself in the Tasks folder.

○ **Arrange tasks:** Go to the View tab and click the buttons in the Arrangement group to organize your task list by Due Date, Type, Importance and so on.

○ **Change views:** Also on the View tab click the Change View button to select your preferred option for organizing your task list, such as by Overdue, Next 7 Days or Prioritized.

Above: The Change View button also has several options for changing the way your task list is organized.

Managing Tasks

○ **Edit a task:** Double-click the task to open the Task window. You can change any of the details or add a related Office document simply by dragging and dropping a file onto the Task window or clicking the Attach File button on the Insert tab.

○ **Mark a task as complete:** Click the check box beside the task in the Tasks window and a grey line is drawn through it.

○ **Delete a task:** Highlight the task and press the Delete button.

MOBILE OUTLOOK

This is the free web-based email service from Microsoft. Using a new Outlook.com account (or one from a previous email service such as @hotmail, @live or @msn) you can connect on the go to your email, calendar and more.

OUTLOOK.COM

To get the best of both worlds use Outlook.com and Outlook together. Use Outlook as your email app when you're at your computer and Outlook.com when you're on the move.

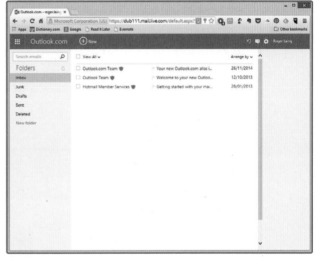

Above: Outlook.com lets you access your email online from the desktop and a variety of mobile devices.

Running Outlook and Outlook.com Together

1. To get your own @outlook.com address go to **www.outlook.com** and click on the Sign up now link.

2. You can then link it to **Outlook 2013** on your computer by going to the File tab and clicking Add Account.

3. The **Add Account** box opens, showing the Auto Account Setup page.

4. Enter your **name**, **email address** and **password**. When Outlook has finished creating the account, click Finish.

Using Outlook.com

○ **Send an email:** Click the + sign inside a circle, and in the window that opens add a subject line and your message, plus the address of the person you're sending it to. Click the Insert button to add attachments or inline pictures. When finished click the Send button.

Above: Go to www.outlook.com to sign up for your own free @outlook.com email address.

○ **Receiving emails:** Open a message and different options appear on the blue bar above:

• **Reply:** Use this to reply to the sender, or select Reply All or Forward from the drop-down list.

• **Delete:** This removes the email.

Above: Once you receive a message, the blue bar in your Inbox offers a range of options for what you can do – such as reply, archive or move the email to a different folder.

Hot Tip

On the go, you can also access a mobile version of Outlook.com through the browser of your tablet or smartphone by going to http://m.mail.live.com.

- **Archive**: This stores the message.

- **Junk**: Use this to mark the email as spam, a scam or worse.

- **Sweep**: Decide how to handle this and future emails from the same address.

Above: The Outlook.com app, like this one for the Android phone, gives access to your online mail wherever you are.

- **Move to**: Organize your messages by moving them to different folders.

Mobile Access

You can access your Outlook.com account from later versions of Windows phones, iOS devices or Android phones, and stay in touch with your email wherever you are.

Right: Your messages in Outlook.com can also be accessed through the browser on your tablet or smartphone.

POWERFUL PRESENTATIONS WITH POWERPOINT

POWERPOINT

PowerPoint presentations are used everywhere – in meetings, lectures and conferences. A poor slideshow is often described as 'Death by PowerPoint'. Here's how to make your presentations dynamic and fun.

WHAT IS POWERPOINT?

PowerPoint is the Microsoft Office program for creating presentations, made up of several slides, which are used by businesses, clubs and other organizations for sales and marketing promotions, training, education and more.

PowerPoint 2013 Window

1 **File tab**: This is where you manage your presentations. From this backstage area you can save, open and print your PowerPoint files.

2 **Quick Access Toolbar**: Available from any screen this has four basic commands – Save, Undo, Repeat and Start from the beginning. Others can be added by clicking the drop-down button next to it.

3 **Ribbon**: Shows the tabs with all the commands for the different actions. Some are contextual tabs, which appear only when you need them, like the Picture Tools Format tab that's added when you insert a picture.

Above: PowerPoint has become the de facto standard for presentation software.

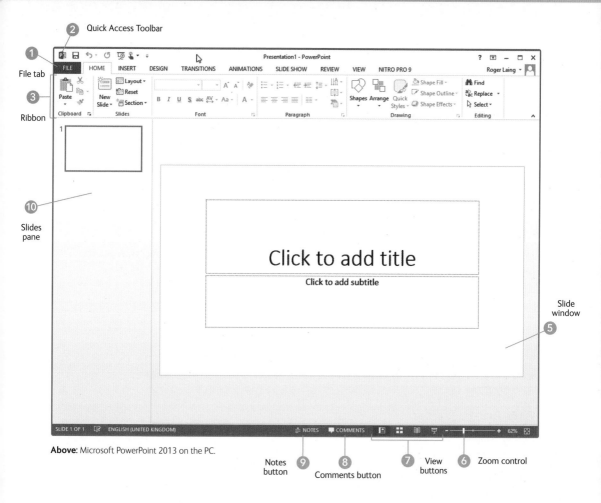

Quick Access Toolbar

File tab

Ribbon

Slides pane

Slide window

Above: Microsoft PowerPoint 2013 on the PC.

Notes button

Comments button

View buttons

Zoom control

4️⃣ **Format pane:** Applies detailed effects to pictures, videos and the like.

5️⃣ **Slide window:** The main space where you see the individual slides in your presentation.

6️⃣ **Zoom control:** For enlarging or reducing the slide.

7️⃣ **View buttons:** For changing how you see your presentation.

⑧ Comments button: Opens a pane where you can add your thoughts on the presentation or see what others have said.

⑨ Notes button: Shows or hides the Notes pane where you can add your commentary for the slide. These notes aren't seen by the audience.

⑩ Slides pane: Shows all the slides in the presentation. Scroll up or down to move through the presentation.

PowerPoint on the Mac

The latest standalone version for Apple Mac computers is PowerPoint 2011. Although its layout is different to the PC version, most of the features are the same.

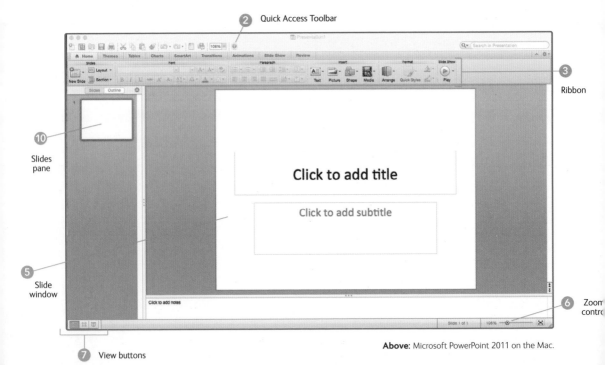

Above: Microsoft PowerPoint 2011 on the Mac.

CREATING A NEW PRESENTATION

PowerPoint presentations are a great way to get your ideas across. There are many templates available for you to choose from, which make it quick and easy to produce very professional-looking slideshows.

Getting Started

To create your presentation in PowerPoint, go to the File tab and select New from the menu. In the window that opens you have several choices:

- **Open a blank presentation**: Design the presentation from scratch, choosing the theme – the colours, layout, fonts and so on – that you want.

- **Select a featured template**: Professionally designed slide layouts by Microsoft with places for you to add text, graphics and images.

Hot Tip

If the Personal tab isn't visible, tell PowerPoint where your templates are stored. In the File tab select Options, then Save and enter the file path in the Default Personal Templates Location box.

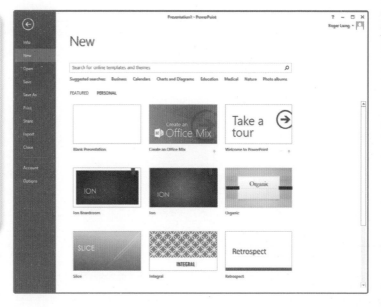

Right: You can choose to create your presentation from scratch, from a professionally designed template or from a previous presentation.

Above: If none of the templates included with PowerPoint is suitable, there are thousands more to search online.

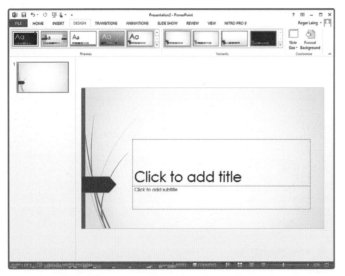

Above: Select your base theme from the Themes gallery on the Design tab.

- **Open a personal template:** You may have a business, school or club template for use in presentations. Select the tab in the main window.

- **Search online for more templates and themes:** Enter a keyword in the search box or select one of the categories underneath and choose from the many templates and themes available at Office.com.

- **Click Open** from the left-hand menu and access a recent PowerPoint presentation.

Choosing Your Theme or Background

You can change the colours and fonts in your theme – which is a pre-packaged design for your slides – with designer-chosen combinations known as Variants:

1.   Go to the **Design** tab.

2. Move your pointer over the designs in the Themes gallery and a **live preview** of how it will look appears in the main slide window.

3. Click on a **theme** to use it as your base.

4. Hover over the **Variants group** and available variants will be previewed in the main window.

5. Click the drop-down button to try out different **colours**, **fonts**, **effects** and **backgrounds**.

Customizing Themes

If none of the designer options appeals, you can go the extra mile and create your own themes, colours and fonts.

Click the View tab and then Slide Master. In the Background group click Colors, Fonts, Effects and Background Styles to customize your slides.

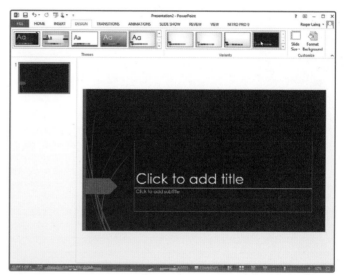

Above: See how you could vary key elements of your theme, like colour, in the Variants section.

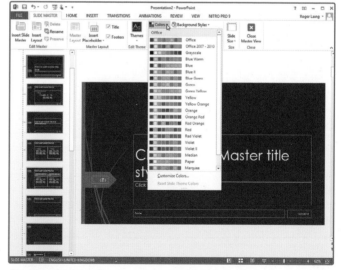

Above: The Slide Master lets you customize your slides with your choice of themes, colours and fonts.

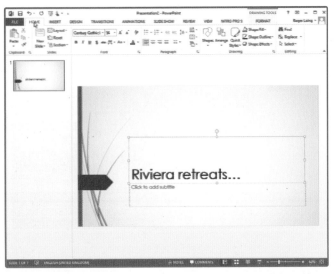

Above: Enter text by overwriting the placeholder instructions Click to add... in the text box.

Above: Change the text size a point at a time using the buttons on the Home tab.

ADDING CONTENT

Once satisfied with the design of your presentation you need to add the content. This means video, animations and sound, as well as text and pictures.

Add Text

The easiest way to enter text is to click in the placeholder text boxes on the slide and start typing.

Change the Look of Your Text

While the theme controls the default size of the text, you can change it on individual slides:

- **Change the font:** Highlight the text and change the font and size you want from the Home tab. If you don't know what size you want, use the two buttons beside the box to increase or decrease font size, a point at a time.

- **Change font colour:** Highlight the text, click the drop-down arrow beside the Font Color button and choose a colour.

○ **Change appearance**: Select the text, go to the Design tab, click Format Background and then in the Format Shape panel choose Text Options. Here you can change the text fill – to a gradually changing colour, pattern or texture – and alter the outline of the words.

○ **Add text effects**: Find and add effects such as shadow or gloss in the Text Effects tab.

Creating Lists

○ Some designs automatically set up text boxes as **items in a list**. Press Enter and another bullet point is added. Press Tab and the bullet point is indented further from the left-hand margin.

○ For a standard bulleted list, select the items in the list, go to the Home tab and click the **Bullets button**. Alternatively, right-click the list, choose Bullets from the menu and choose the bullet style from the pop-up menu.

Above: Change the appearance of text by filling it with patterns, textures or colour gradients.

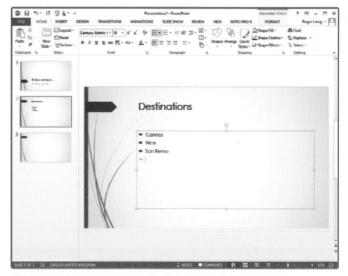

Above: Some themes come with text already formatted as bullet-pointed lists.

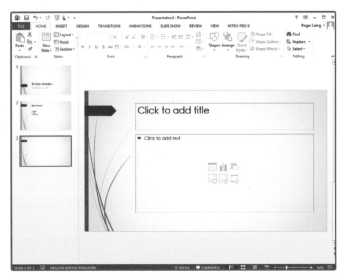

Above: The Content box lets you enter text or choose one of the six pre-formatted content options by clicking the relevant button.

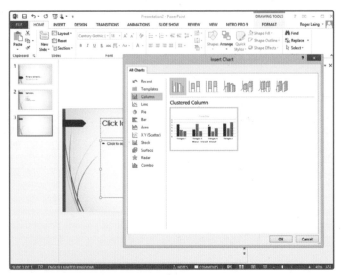

Above: The Insert Chart dialog box lets you choose the type of chart that you require.

○ For a numbered list, follow the same process but choose the **Numbering button**.

Adding Other Content

Each template comes with a selection of slide layouts. These are pre-formatted designs with placeholder boxes for different types of content.

○ **Text box**: For entering titles and other text, as above.

○ **Content box**: Lets you click to add text. Once you do, the other content buttons disappear. Alternatively, click one of these content buttons to open a new window with the relevant options:

• **Insert Table**: Click this and select the number of columns and rows required.

• **Insert Chart**: Lets you choose the sort of chart you want, such as a column or bar chart, and previews how it will look.

Hot Tip

To remove bullets or numbers, highlight the list, click the drop-down arrow beside the Bullets or Numbering buttons and select None.

- **Insert a SmartArt Graphic**: Different-coloured shapes can be used to brighten up lists or illustrations.

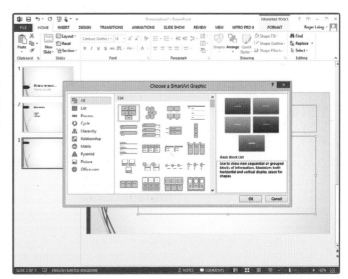

Above: Choose a SmartArt Graphic to add colourful boxes and illustrations to your presentations.

- **Pictures**: Browse your computer to find the picture(s) to insert.

- **Online Pictures**: Search for pictures online, at Office.com or on your OneDrive account.

- **Insert Video**: Lets you browse and add video clips from your computer, OneDrive, YouTube or even some social networks, like Facebook.

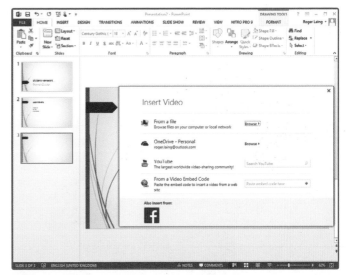

Above: Insert Video lets you add film from sites like YouTube or from your computer or OneDrive online storage account.

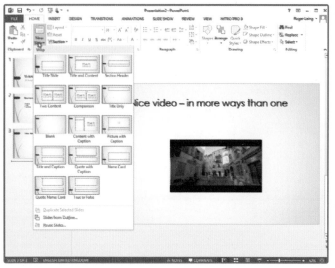

Above: When inserting a slide, select which type of placeholder box – title box, text box, content box or a combination of boxes – that best suits the purpose of the slide.

Inserting a Slide

1. In **Normal view** select the slide in the Slides panel on the left.

2. On the Home or Insert tab click the **New Slide button**.

3. In the drop-down list you can see the **various layouts** available, with their mixture of text and content placeholders.

4. Click the one that offers the **best combination**.

Changing View

There are several ways to view your slides:

Hot Tip

You can change views either using the View buttons on the Status bar or by clicking the appropriate button on the View tab.

○ **Normal**: Thumbnails of your slide appear in the Slides pane on the left with the slide in the main window. The Notes pane is also at the bottom of the screen for you to add comments.

○ **Outline View**: This is handiest when working on the text as it shows just the words on each slide.

○ **Slide Sorter**: Best for organizing slides. It shows numbered thumbnails of all the slides (use the zoom slider on the Status bar to change the size of the thumbnails):

- To **move** a slide in this view, select it and just drag and drop into a new position.

- To **delete** slides, select them, right-click and select Delete Slide.

○ **Notes Page**: Opens the Notes pane to see your written commentary for the presentation.

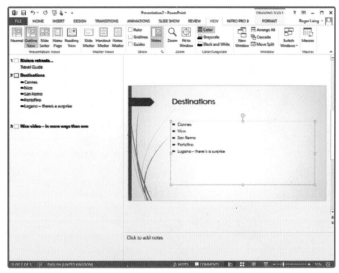

Above: Outline View is best for working on the presentation's text.

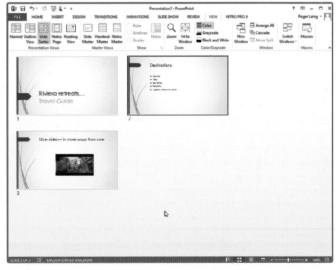

Above: The Slide Sorter view makes it easy to arrange or delete slides.

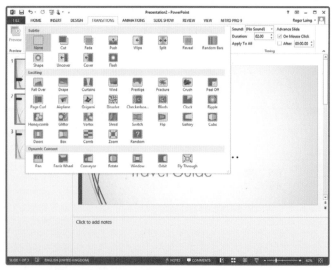

Step 5: The Transitions gallery offers many effects for moving between slides.

○ **Reading View**: Allows you to proofread each slide, with a single slide onscreen and buttons for moving between slides in the presentation.

TRANSITION EFFECTS

For a more dynamic presentation you can add special transitioning effects – like fade or push – as one slide moves to the next, or add animations, such as bullets zooming in, one at a time, on a slide.

Step-by-Step: Adding Transitions Between Slides

1. **Select** the slides where you want the transition.

2. Go to the Transitions tab and the **Transition to This Slide** group.

3. Click the **Transition Styles** button to open the gallery.

4. The gallery includes **Subtle** transitions (such as the traditional fade or push), **Exciting** (like Airplane or Dissolve), or **Dynamic** (such as the Ferris Wheel or Fly Through). There are many others.

5. Click the **Preview** button to see the transition applied to the slide.

6. Click the **Effects** button and you can choose different options for the transition, such as applying it from the right or left of the slide.

Step 6: Once you have chosen the transition the Effects button offers further options to customize it.

7. Press the **Sound** button if you want to have a sound effect to mark the transition.

8. In the **Duration** box mark how long you want the transition to take.

9. Click the **Apply To All** button if you want the same transition for all slides in the presentation.

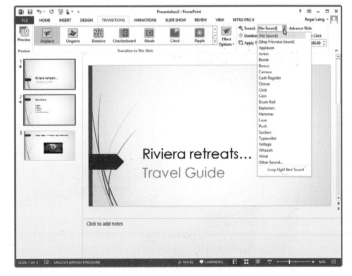

Step 7: There are various sounds you can add along with the transition.

Above: The Animation gallery provides several ways to animate the actions on individual slides.

Animating Slides

1. For pre-built animations go to the **Animations** tab.

2. Select the **element** on the slide you want to animate, such as a text box with a bulleted list.

3. Click the Animation button and select the **style** you want from the gallery.

4. Click the **Preview** button to see the effect applied and click the Effect Options button to alter your animation.

Hot Tip

To remove a transition just select the relevant slides and select None from the Transitions gallery.

POWERPOINT ON THE GO

Need to add an extra slide or make a last-minute change to some of the content in your presentation? You can do this with PowerPoint apps for tablets and smartphones or PowerPoint Online, accessible from any PC or mobile device with a browser.

MOBILE POWERPOINT

While most mobile PowerPoint apps and the online service have limited features compared with the desktop version, they do enable you to carry out last-minute tweaks to your presentation.

Tablets and Smartphones

- Windows Phones come with the touch-optimized **Office Mobile app** installed, which lets you view and edit PowerPoint presentations as well as Word and Excel documents.

- There is now a standalone **PowerPoint app** for the iPad and iPhone (also currently available in free beta for Android tablets and planned for Android phones).

- With the app you can **view**, **create** and **edit** presentations for free, but there are several premium features that are only available with an Office 365 subscription. These include adding custom colours to shapes, inserting WordArt and adding or modifying charts.

Hot Tip

Windows tablets are the exception to the rule, as they run the full desktop version of PowerPoint. However, it has been adapted for easier use with a touchscreen.

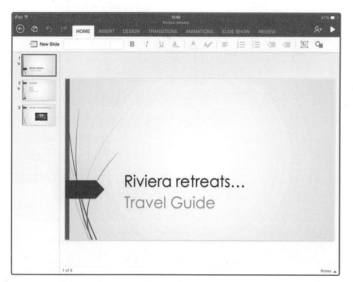

Above: The PowerPoint iPad app is good for last-minute alterations to presentations.

PowerPoint Online

- Sign in through the **browser** on any PC or mobile device, using your (free) Microsoft account, and use the PowerPoint Online web app to create and edit your presentations.

- Although it has fewer features than the desktop version, it does include **Transitions** and **Animations**. Your file is automatically saved as you work to your OneDrive.

- For the full PowerPoint experience, you can open the presentation for **editing** in the desktop version of PowerPoint (if available).

- You can also **share** your presentations and invite others to add comments.

Right: Although PowerPoint Online is more limited than the desktop version, it does include Transitions and Animations.

NOTE-TAKING AND MORE WITH OTHER OFFICE PROGRAMS

ONENOTE

Where do you put all the information you need, whether it's a web page, Office document, photo or a sudden idea that has come to you? OneNote lets you store and organize your notes from a variety of sources.

WHAT IS ONENOTE?

OneNote is the perfect place to store your notes, which can be combined to create new documents or used to brainstorm ideas and projects.

Organizing Your Notebooks

- **Notebook:** This is the file that contains all the notes for a project, such as a notebook called 'Summer Party' for organizing an event. Each notebook appears in the Notebook pane, so you can move easily between them.

- **Sections:** There can be many sections within a notebook and each section can have a number of pages. In the example above, you could have a section for each possible venue with several pages covering its advantages.

Left: From web clippings to scribbled notes, store your ideas together in one place with OneNote.

○ **Section groups**: These make it easier to find sections when you have too many, so for example several possible venues for the summer party could be put together in a section group labelled 'Location'.

○ **Pages**: For writing and storing notes. When you select a section the pages appear on the right in the Page pane. Select an entry in the pane and it opens in the main Page window.

Above: There are several different layers, from note to notebook, in which you can organize your thoughts and ideas.

○ **Notes**: These can be written on pages by simply clicking and starting to type.

OneNote Window

1 **File tab**: Click here to access the backstage view, where you open, create, share and print your notes as well as change settings.

2 **Section tabs**: Show open sections.

3 **Section groups**: For holding several sections.

4 **Search box**: For finding your notes.

5 **Page pane**: Select an entry to open the page in the main Page window.

6 **Create pages**: Click the Add Page icon.

Hot Tip

To group sections together, right-click any section tab and click New Section group. To add a section to the group just drag their tab over the group icon.

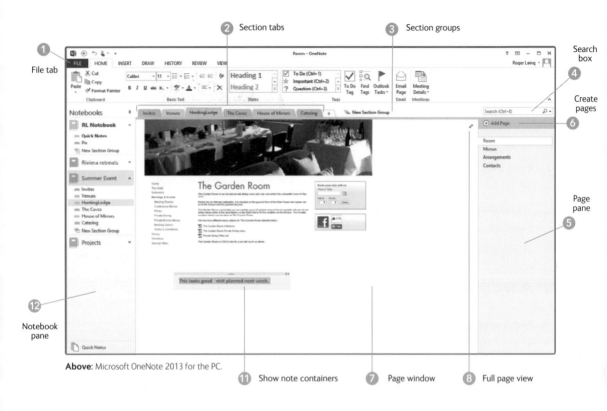

② Section tabs

③ Section groups

① File tab

Search box **④**

Create pages **⑥**

⑫ Notebook pane

Page pane **⑤**

Above: Microsoft OneNote 2013 for the PC.

⑪ Show note containers

⑦ Page window

⑧ Full page view

⑦ **Page window:** Shows the page with notes.

⑧ **Full page view:** Click the double arrow to enlarge your page.

⑨ **Jottings:** If you have a touchscreen, add handwritten ideas or drawings to your notes.

⑩ **Tags:** These provide a quick way to prioritize your notes.

Hot Tip

OneNote automatically saves everything so you can concentrate on your notes and ideas and nothing else.

11 Show note containers: Hover over the text and the container shows. Click the top bar to move it around the screen.

12 Notebook pane: Shows all the notebooks.

Send to OneNote

In Windows this can be opened by pressing the Windows button+N and gives you three quick ways to add notes: Screen Clipping will add anything on screen – such as a web page – to OneNote; Send to OneNote is a quick way to add information from other Office documents; while the third option lets you add a New Quick Note.

OneNote for Mac

Although the Mac desktop app doesn't have all the rich features of the Windows version, it does let you copy and paste formatted content, drag and drop pictures, import email and more.

Above: Screen Clipping lets you select an area of a web page and save it to a specified location in OneNote.

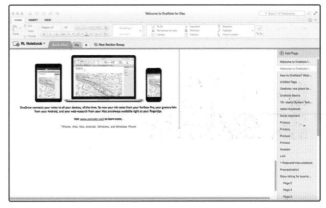

Above: The Mac desktop version of OneNote doesn't have all the rich features of the Windows version.

You can also clip web pages to OneNote using a bookmarklet that works in most major browsers (for Mac and PC).

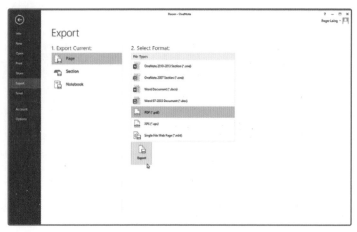

Above: From the File tab you can choose to export a note – or complete notebook – to share with someone who may not have the program.

Sharing Notes

Share a snapshot of a note – or entire notebook – with someone who doesn't have the program. Go to the File tab, click Export and select the required format.

OneNote on the Go

To make OneNote your digital notebook of choice there are apps for Windows tablets and phones, iPads, iPhones, Android phones and the free web app OneNote Online. As everything is synced to OneDrive you can always have the latest version of your notes to hand.

Above: OneNote for iPad offers many of the features of the desktop version.

Left: Use the OneNote smartphone app to keep your notes with you on the go.

PUBLISHER

Microsoft Publisher 2013 is desktop publishing software that provides a quick and simple way to produce stunning, professional-looking publications.

WHAT TO DO WITH PUBLISHER

The range of publications you can make is virtually endless – from a simple greetings card to a newsletter, magazine or catalogue. The downside is that it is only available on Windows PCs.

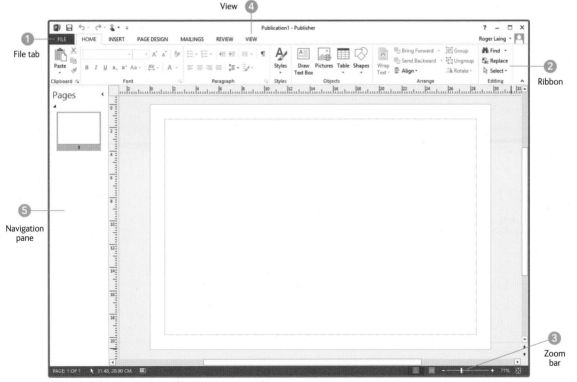

Above: Microsoft Publisher 2013 for the PC.

Publisher Window

1 **File tab**: Has the backstage area where you create, open, save and manage your publication files.

2 **Ribbon**: With different commands grouped on the various tabs. Among the most important are:

- **Home**: Pictures button lets you add images to your publication.

- **Insert**: To add text boxes, pictures and shapes.

- **Page Design**: Lets you change templates, page sizes and layouts.

- **Mailings**: For adding mail and email fields that let you customize publications with personal information, such as names and addresses.

- **Review**: For checking spelling and proofing your publications.

- **View**: Changes how you see your publication.

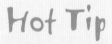

Hot Tip

When you add several pictures Publisher puts them in a special working – scratch – area. From here drag and drop the pictures where you want them or drag them off again if they look wrong.

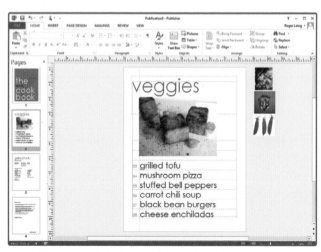

Above: Pictures can be dragged and dropped on and off the page.

3 **Zoom bar**: Use the slider bar to zoom in or out of your publication pages.

4 **View**: Switch between single page and double-page spreads.

5 **Navigation pane**: This is the easiest way to scroll through the pages in your publication and add or delete them.

Using a Template

Every publication starts with a template. Click the File tab and select New to open the templates gallery. To use one of the pre-designed publications, select one of the templates shown under Featured and click Create. To build a publication from scratch, select Blank.

Add Pictures

On the Home tab click Pictures then Insert Pictures, which lets you find images on your computer, or navigate to Online Pictures where you can get photos from the web or the Office.com gallery.

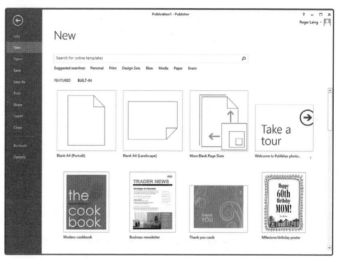

Above: The New page on the File tab offers a choice of templates plus a variety of blank page sizes to cater for different-sized publications.

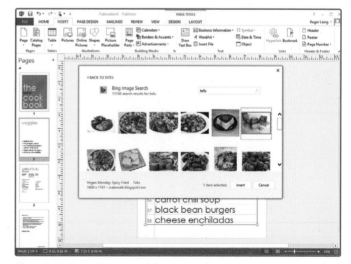

Above: Online Pictures lets you search for relevant images on the web.

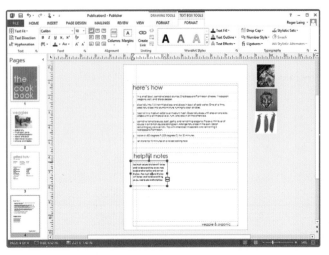

Above: The ellipsis on the right of the text box shows there is too much content to display. Either enlarge the box or add a second box for the text to flow into.

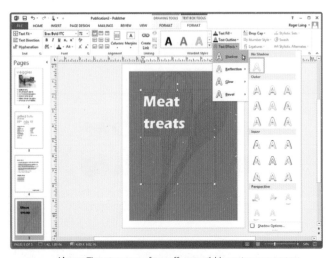

Above: There is a range of text effects available to give your content more impact.

Add Text

1. First add the text box to hold the text. On the Home tab press the **Draw Text Box** button. Drag the cursor on the page where you want the text box. Type your text.

2. If your text is **too long**, an **ellipsis** appears in the bottom-right corner. To accommodate the extra words, drag the handles of your text box to make it bigger.

3. Alternatively, **link** it to a second text box by first creating a new text box, then clicking the ellipsis and the cursor changes to a pitcher. Move this to the new text box and click.

4. The text will now **flow** into the second text box.

Text Effects

Make your text stand out with special effects, such as shadows, glows or reflections. Highlight the text and from the Text Box Tools that appear on the Format tab select Text Effects.

ACCESS

Access lets you create desktop databases for recording and organizing everything from contacts to business accounts. It is only available for the PC.

USING ACCESS

The pre-defined databases available as templates in Access make it easy to get started with databases that can track your charitable contributions, projects, events and much more.

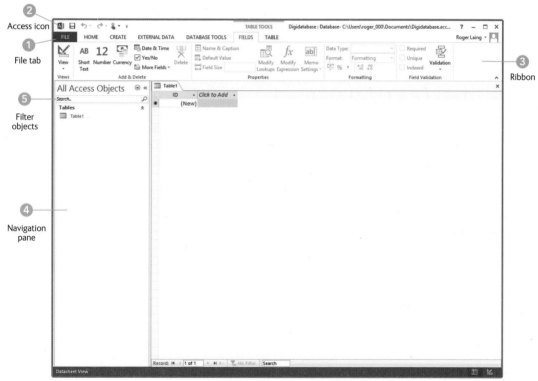

Above: Microsoft Access 2013 for the PC.

Access Window

1 File tab: Lets you manage your databases, including encrypting, compacting or repairing them, as well as opening, saving and printing your files.

2 Access icon: Click this to resize the window or to close the database.

3 Ribbon: Includes various tabs that group similar commands together. The tabs are:

- **Home**: Where you see the database records, copy and paste data, and sort and filter your information.

- **Create**: Where you add tables, run queries on the database and set up reports.

- **External Data**: Lets you import data and link to external sources.

- **Database Tools**: To help you keep the database running smoothly, repair or compact the database, and analyze or move data.

> ## Hot Tip
>
> To add data go to the External Data tab and you can copy and paste from other Office programs, like Excel or Word, or you can import or link to data from other sources, such as a web page or SharePoint file.

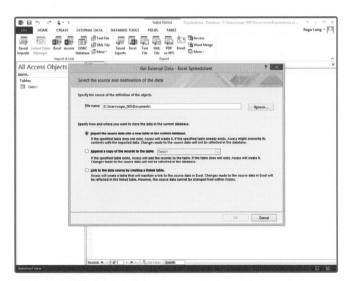

Above: To speed up the process of adding information to the database, you can import data from an existing Excel spreadsheet or other source.

④ **Navigation pane**: View and use All Access Objects in the database. These objects include the tables that store the data; queries that find or sort data; forms that let you input data; reports that display the results of your queries, such as a financial summary; Macros, which are scripts for doing a task; and Modules, where you can write your own scripts and programs.

⑤ **Filter objects**: Type a keyword in the Search box to find the relevant objects in the database.

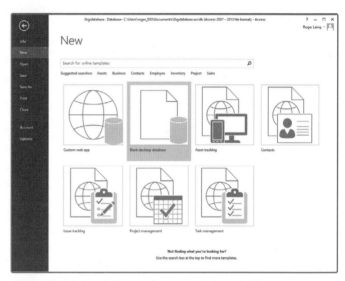

Above: A blank desktop database template comes complete with tables, queries and built-in reports.

Getting Started with Access

1. In Access go to the File tab and select **New**.

2. Choose a **desktop database** as this has built-in tables, queries, forms and reports to use.

3. Enter a **name** for your database, accept the default **location** or change it and click Create.

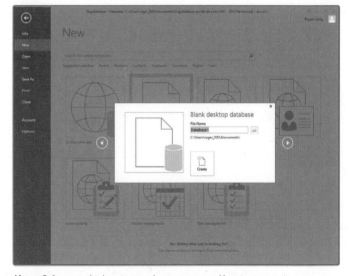

Above: Before your database is created, enter a name and location to store it.

USEFUL WEBSITES AND FURTHER READING

WEBSITES

www.blogs.microsoft.com
Official Microsoft blog regularly updated with news on business and software developments.

www.dummies.com/how-to/computers-software/ms-office.html
The official online portal for the popular and entertaining *For Dummies* series of books, including a section on Microsoft Office.

www.gcflearnfree.org/office
Online tutorials for all versions of Microsoft Office.

www.msofficeforums.com
Forum covering questions and responses about all Microsoft Office applications.

www.office.microsoft.com
Microsoft's official website offering how-to articles, downloads, templates, training and advice on all Microsoft Office Applications.

www.ozgrid.com/Excel/
A list of Excel formulas, plus tips and tricks on how to use them.

www.store.office.com
App store for Microsoft Office on the go.

www.wordbanter.com
A forum that focuses on Word and Word-related topics.

FURTHER READING

Microsoft Office: 2013 Edition (Microsoft Official Academic Course), John Wiley & Sons, 2014

Bott, Ed and Siechert, Carl, *Microsoft Office Inside Out: 2013 Edition*, Microsoft Press, 2013

Bucki, Lisa A., et al, *Office 2013 Bible: The Comprehensive Tutorial Resource*, John Wiley & Sons, 2013

Conner, Nancy and MacDonald, Matthew, *Office 2013: The Missing Manual*, O'Reilly Media, 2013

Johnson, Steve, *Brilliant Office 2013 (Brilliant Computing): What you Need to Know and How to Do it*, Pearson, 2013

Laing, Roger, *Microsoft Excel Basics*, Flame Tree Publishing Ltd, 2015

Laing, Roger, *Microsoft Word Basics*, Flame Tree Publishing Ltd, 2015

Price, Michael, *Office 2013 in Easy Steps*, In Easy Steps Limited, 2013

Smith, Chris, *Microsoft PowerPoint Made Easy*, Flame Tree Publishing Ltd, 2013

Wang, Wallace, *Office 2013 for Dummies*, For Dummies, 2013

INDEX